PRAISE FOR *Bright Spots & Landmines*

"A superb and compelling read... In these pages you will find years of lessons learned and tips you can immediately apply in your own life with diabetes. Adam's personal journey can teach us all to find our Bright Spots, no matter what diabetes throws at us."

DR. FRANCINE KAUFMAN | Author of *Diabesity*; Endocrinologist at Children's Hospital Los Angeles; Chief Medical Officer at Medtronic Diabetes

"When Adam has advice, I listen. There are few people in the world who have more visibility into the cutting edge of diabetes. *Bright Spots & Landmines* is an incredible resource from a true champion for people with diabetes."

DR. AARON KOWALSKI | Chief Mission Officer at JDRF; 33 years living with diabetes

"For me, this is the most anticipated book ever for people living with diabetes."

JOHN SJÖLUND | Founder/CEO of Timesulin; 32 years living with diabetes

"When I picked up this book, my A1c was 9.3%. After just a month, I'm down to 8.3% and still falling! Every person with diabetes, young or old, should read *Bright Spots & Landmines*. I plan to be one of Adam's biggest success stories."

STEVE MALLINSON | 24 years living with diabetes

"Living with diabetes, we all have good days and not-so-good days. Adam's book is an essential guide on how to make the good days more frequent, more predictable, and a lot more fun."

JAMES S. HIRSCH | Author of *Cheating Destiny*; 36 years living with diabetes

"A must-read for anyone living with diabetes and those who care for them. After 35 years with diabetes, I still took some very valuable lessons from Adam. No matter where you are in your diabetes journey, life will be easier after this read. I guarantee you will learn something new, get inspired, and feel more empowered."

PHIL SOUTHERLAND | Author of *Not Dead Yet*; Co-founder of Team Novo Nordisk and the Team Type 1 Foundation; 35 years living with diabetes

"This book is exceptional – every single page has actions you can apply to your own life to make it better. You would have to read ten good books to pick up the advice that Adam packs into this one. I give this book my strongest endorsement and recommend it to everyone with diabetes."

DAVID EDELMAN | Founder of *Diabetes Daily*

"Our son dropped his A1c from 11.1% to 4.9% in three months! Following Adam's advice made it easy and makes living with diabetes so much less stressful. This inspiring book is a goldmine of helpful information, especially on foods to eat. Chia pudding has changed our lives!"

SARITA LISA | Mother of Aden (diagnosed November 2016)

"Adam understands more about living with diabetes than almost anyone I know, both from trial and error with his own blood sugar levels as well as through interactions with many leaders in the diabetes community. *Bright Spots & Landmines* takes his experience to another level. This book shares exactly what I teach my patients and does so beautifully. What a gift."

DR. ANNE PETERS | Director, USC Clinical Diabetes Program and Professor, Keck School of Medicine of USC

"Adam artfully uses personal experience, positive psychology, science, and common sense to teach and to tame diabetes for his readers. His storytelling is masterful and the sensitivity in his approach is profound. This book is what I needed yesterday and what I still need today in my diabetes life."

DR. NICOLE JOHNSON | Founder of Students With Diabetes; Miss America 1999; 24 years living with diabetes

"I've lived with diabetes for over 50 years, and when I get *diaTribe*, I read Adam's column before all the others. This impressive book shares Adam's story and tons of specific, useful tips for managing my blood sugar. I completely agree with his approach."

NANCY CRANE | Over 50 years living with diabetes

"Thank you, Adam, for crafting a book that inspires, educates, and does not intimidate. The tide of well-being in the diabetes community rises with this book."

KERRI SPARLING | Author of *Balancing Diabetes*; blogger at SixUntilMe.com; 30 years living with diabetes

"*Bright Spots & Landmines* is just what the doctor ordered: easy-to-understand, actionable advice to help people with diabetes live well. Adam will guide you through food choices that make blood glucose management easier, strategies for making exercise an integral part of even your busiest day, and tips for adopting a positive mindset. Whether you live with type 1 diabetes, type 2 diabetes, or have been told that you have prediabetes, this book will help you in your journey to a life well lived."

JEFF HITCHCOCK | Founder and President of Children with Diabetes

"*Bright Spots & Landmines* is wonderful work! I loved this book's positive focus, honesty, and real-life tips. A must-read!"

SCOTT JOHNSON | Blogger at ScottsDiabetes.com; Communications Lead at mySugr USA; 37 years living with diabetes

"All I can say is: 'Wow!' I can't wait to get this into the hands of my patients. Is this book highly actionable? You bet! I am certain that A1c's will drop, time-in-range will increase, and diabetes burden will be lifted as readers with type 1 and type 2 diabetes apply the Bright Spots and avoid the Landmines."

DR. DANIEL DESALVO | Endocrinologist at Texas Children's Hospital; 17 years living with diabetes

"Adam has put his brain, heart, and soul into this project. *Bright Spots & Landmines* is an amazing book filled with gems for people with diabetes and their caregivers."

GLORIA YEE | Certified Diabetes Educator at California Pacific Medical Center; 30 years living with diabetes

"Adam's guidance and advice in this book is, in my opinion, far more valuable than what you'll get at your next diabetes check-up. Anyone looking to expand their understanding of diabetes management, nutrition, exercise, and beyond will absolutely benefit from reading this book – even if you've had diabetes for 10 or more years!"

GINGER VIEIRA | Author of *Pregnancy with Type 1 Diabetes, Dealing with Diabetes Burnout, Emotional Eating with Diabetes,* and *Your Diabetes Science Experiment*; 18 years living with diabetes

BRIGHT SP☀TS

& LANDMINES

The **DIABETES GUIDE**

I Wish Someone Had Handed Me

by Adam Brown

Foreword by Kelly L. Close

The diaTribe Foundation
804 Haight Street
San Francisco, CA 94117

www.diaTribe.org

Cover, interior design, and photography by Priscilla Leung
Headshot by Joseph Fanvu Photography

ISBN-13 (Color, mmol/l): 9780999792704

ISBN-13 (B&W, mmol/l): 9780999792711

The opinions in this book reflect the research and ideas of the author, but are not intended to substitute for the services of a trained healthcare provider. Consult with your healthcare provider before engaging in any diet, drug, or exercise regimen. The author and the diaTribe Foundation disclaim responsibility for any adverse effects resulting directly or indirectly from information contained in this book.

A NOTE FROM ADAM

Bright Spots & Landmines shares my diabetes journey, focused on the food, mindset, exercise, and sleep strategies that have dramatically improved my blood sugars, state of mind, overall health, and quality of life.

Please do not interpret this book as medical advice, and please consult a healthcare provider before making big changes to your routine – especially if you use insulin. The blood glucose targets and insulin dose changes should be individualized based on your needs.

Several products I use are mentioned in this book. I have not received any compensation for writing about them.

All proceeds from sales of *Bright Spots & Landmines* benefit The diaTribe Foundation, a 501(c)(3) nonprofit dedicated to improving the lives of people with diabetes and prediabetes, and advocating for action.

CONTENTS

FOREWORD

Some years ago, I happened to see Adam on New Year's Eve. He was wearing a Fitbit, a relatively new device at the time, and I asked if I could take a look. And there it was – Adam had already walked 11,000 steps that day! Just because it was December 31 didn't mean it was time to kick back. I wondered what his week looked like; surely the holiday season would have complicated his schedule. Wrong again: he had racked up 10,300 steps on average each of the past seven days. How about the month? He clocked in at 12,000 steps a day, on average. Okay, anyone can have a great four weeks, but what did the year look like?

You guessed it. He averaged 10,004 steps a day!

Adam has been my friend and colleague for seven years, and without even looking at his Fitbit, I can tell you he hasn't missed a step.

Someone who is that hyper-disciplined, that dedicated to his own health, can be intimidating. You feel as if no matter how hard you try, you can never measure up to this other person. But Adam sends out the exact opposite vibe. I see his passion to eat right, to exercise regularly, and to take care of his health every day, but he is just as interested in your physical and emotional well-being as his own.

For example, I sometimes feel discouraged after looking at my blood glucose, and I talk to Adam, who reminds me how challenging diabetes really is, how hard I'm working, and how well I'm actually doing.

"You're such a good parent," he also tells me. Or, "You're such a good boss, or colleague, or friend."

His words always make me feel better.

That's why I couldn't be more delighted that Adam has written this book. Wow, has it been an exciting process to be part of! You will discover many helpful ways to find "Diabetes Bright Spots" and avoid "Diabetes Landmines," and you will also have a very good friend in Adam. Besides diabetes, the only other chronic conditions Adam has are perpetual good humor and a love of learning. Conscientious and self-effacing, he wears his optimism as durably as he tracks his steps, believing that education and encouragement are what we need to live longer and better lives. Adam's faith in these tools animates every page of this book.

For many years now, Adam's immensely popular column in *diaTribe* (Adam's Corner) has been a herald for life-transforming tips on managing diabetes. He knows more about diabetes technology and digital health than anyone on this planet (seriously!), and he writes with equal parts expertise and empathy.

Consider sleep, which is one of the very important but often overlooked issues in diabetes care. Now, sleep is not really *my* thing, and I know I don't get enough of it, but only after reading Adam's chapter on sleep – and how seven hours of it can actually help produce better blood sugars the next day – did I fully realize why this is essential to my own health. Similar revelations can be found in this book on what to eat to minimize blood sugar swings, how to tackle exercise highs and lows and barriers, and why five mindful minutes in the morning (or one!) can make a difference all day. And so much more.

Trust me, Adam's narrative is so grounded and so caring, mixing science with personal stories, that after reading this book, you will find yourself walking after meals or changing your restaurant orders. You might also, as Adam describes, find why in-range blood sugars help you *today*; engage your friends and family in your own care so that it's more doable; and focus on consistency and routine, not just outcomes.

I love that this book is laser-focused on *action* – and that Adam has been unwavering in his goal: helping people with all kinds of diabetes through small but meaningful steps.

Can *anyone* read this book and improve some aspect of their life? Whether you have type 1, type 2, or even prediabetes, my answer is an emphatic "Yes!" *Bright Spots & Landmines* will make you smarter about your diabetes, more confident in your care, more hopeful in your future, and absolutely certain that you are not alone in this journey.

Please share this book with friends and family too – even if they don't have diabetes! It will help us create a healthier nation and world, one of our main goals here at The diaTribe Foundation.

And one more thing. Buy a tracking device and count your steps. It's more fun than counting carbs (do that too!), and every day of the year – even the last day – will be a *Bright Spot*.

KELLY L. CLOSE
Founder and Chair, The diaTribe Foundation

MY STORY, WHY BRIGHT SPOTS & LANDMINES, AND HOW TO USE THIS BOOK

"The price of light is less than the cost of darkness."

ARTHUR C. NIELSEN

We have too much darkness in diabetes – negativity, confusion, frustration, exhaustion, blame, guilt, and fear. For those of us living with diabetes and the people we love, the cost of this darkness is high. We often don't know what to do, aren't doing what we "should" be doing, feel bad about what we are doing, or are told we're getting it wrong.

We can do so much better!

This is a hopeful book about making type 1 and type 2 diabetes easier, and the premise is simple:

Identify what works and focus on doing those things more often (Diabetes Bright Spots).

What's going well in my diabetes that I should keep doing? What happens on my best days? What foods and decisions keep my blood glucose in the tight range of 4-8 mmol/l (70-140 mg/dl*)? What puts me in a positive frame of mind? How can I do *more* of these things each day?

Uncover what doesn't work and find ways to do those things less often (Diabetes Landmines**).**

> What decisions do I make repeatedly that explode into out-of-range blood glucose values over 11 mmol/l or less than 4 mmol/l? What happens on my most challenging days with diabetes? What choices do I always regret? What repeatedly brings on negative feelings? How can I do *fewer* of these things each day?

What you are about to read is the actionable guide I wish I was handed at diagnosis, focused on the Diabetes Bright Spots that have most improved my blood sugars and mental outlook, and the Diabetes Landmines I'm always working to avoid. Each chapter – Food, Mindset, Exercise, and Sleep – shares exactly how I increase my Bright Spots and steer clear of my Landmines. This framework has proven remarkably powerful for me, particularly because Bright Spots are so useful and so often ignored.

Everything in this book has made a difference in my life with diabetes, and nearly all my suggestions include a small step that can be taken immediately. Ironically – and painfully – some of the most effective strategies are the *opposite* of what I was told at diagnosis, particularly around what to eat and the mental side of diabetes.

I'm excited to share my journey with you, and far more important, I hope this book is valuable to you – whether you were just diagnosed or have had diabetes for 50 years. There are hundreds of effective tools, tips, and questions in here, but even one small change can make a difference today.

---

* In this international version of the book, I've used "mmol/l" alone in most cases for better readability. Readers that prefer mg/dl units can do an exact conversation by multiplying the mmol/l number by 18. For instance, 4 mmol/l = 72 mg/dl, and 8 mmol/l = 144 mg/dl. For simplicity, anytime you see "4-8 mmol/l", insert "70-140 mg/dl."

WHY I WROTE THIS BOOK

For the last six years, I've had the privilege of writing at *diaTribe*, where our mission is to help improve the lives of people with diabetes and prediabetes. I have written over half a million words on the latest advances and research, and I have covered leading thinkers at hundreds of diabetes conferences from Melbourne to San Francisco to Dubai.

Living well with diabetes, I've learned, comes down to a handful of strategies: relentlessly learning and experimenting to find what works for *me*, using glucose data to help me make better decisions, policing my own negative mindset, optimizing my habits to put more things on auto-pilot, and finding support.

But 15 years ago when I was diagnosed, all of this was foreign to me.

I grew up in rural New Jersey as the oldest of six children. I always believed, from a very young age, in the power of hard work and hustle. I played basketball outside in our driveway in the ice and snow, pushing through the cold to constantly improve. I also had an unwavering belief in the power of knowledge as a vehicle for self-improvement, and I remember Googling things like "How do I increase my vertical jump?" or "How do I improve my dribbling?" As a small and scrawny basketball player, I figured these skills might give me an edge. I would go down into our basement and do hours of drills and hundreds of bodyweight squats, jumps, and calf raises. School was never a problem either; I did whatever it took to get good grades, and my mom never had to bug me to do my work. Self-motivation and discipline were part of my identity.

So when I look back on my diabetes diagnosis, that drive to work hard and constantly improve should have served me well. But the tools were not as good back then, and the instructions on what to do were poor.

I remember feeling shocked and crying at the news – "You have diabetes" – and most of that time is a blur. But I do remember struggling mightily, and I certainly recall feeling like a failure at every doctor's appointment.

I checked my blood glucose (**"BG"**) around four times per day, rarely finding myself in an ideal range. My A1c was far too high at 8%-9%, and the daily swings from 2.5 mmol/l to 17 mmol/l put me at high risk of seizures from extreme low BGs (hypoglycemia) and long-term damage from extreme high BGs (hyperglycemia).

I was oblivious to these cold, hard facts – the *future* threat of "complications" is not a good motivator today, particularly for someone newly diagnosed. Plus, I didn't really know how to get better or what to do differently.

I had a terrifying episode of severe hypoglycemia in those initial months following diagnosis – I took too much insulin at lunch, passed out, and woke up with paramedics around me. Insulin is a very dangerous drug; no one made that clear enough, and no one told me how to make it safer. Perhaps this should have served as a wake-up call to take diabetes more seriously, but in reality, I just felt embarrassed.

The food advice I got at diagnosis was unquestionably the biggest problem, and in retrospect, a true travesty: "You can eat what you want, as long as you take insulin for it." That was a blank check not to change my diet at all, so I didn't: sleeves of crackers, triple cheeseburgers with fries, stacks of cookies, plates of pasta the size of my head – you get the idea. As my mom told me recently, "We were a carb-centric family and always had a treat after supper!"

Those choices didn't seem like a problem at the time, but they translated into large, haphazardly estimated insulin doses followed by many highs, lows, and dangerous glucose swings. What I was doing was dangerous, but as the oldest of six kids, I felt confident I could handle it. Responsibility was my middle name: I grew up without a father figure, which added extra pressure to be the man of the house. In the case of diabetes, unfortunately, being responsible isn't enough to achieve in-range blood sugars.

One day we got takeout – a foot-long ham and turkey sandwich – and I proceeded to chomp it down soon after we got home. Then reality hit: "Wait, I now have diabetes and was supposed to take insulin for these carbs!" I freaked out, recalling the question that raced through my mind after diagnosis: "What's going to happen to me?!"

Nothing did *in that moment*, of course. I took the insulin and carried on with my day. My blood sugar probably went sky high, but I would have had no idea at the time – checking it four times per day didn't give me nearly enough data to learn and make changes.

No one told us back then that white bread is a nightmare for dosing insulin.

No one warned us that eating 92 grams of carbs at once is a huge glucose load in a condition with one big challenge: an inability to deal with huge glucose loads.

Reflecting back, I'm simply glad I survived all the wild, uninformed guesses we took each day. I don't fault my mom or myself; I fault the tools we had in 2001 and the lack of useful, specific advice we received on what to do. In diabetes, the little stuff really matters, the little stuff is easy to forget, and botching the little stuff can lead to serious problems.

The great news is that these challenges can be avoided, and this book is about how to do that.

Six years ago, three positive events happened in quick succession, and these Bright Spots changed my diabetes for the better – and unquestionably, the trajectory of my life.

First, I started learning about nutrition and eating fewer carbohydrates, which subtracted most of those highs and lows, dangerously big insulin doses, and worries. I also became close friends with a bodybuilder, who showed me first-hand what better food choices can do.

 Second, I nervously joined a small organization, Close Concerns, as a summer intern in 2010. I figured it might be fun to learn and write about diabetes for a few months, even though the vision of writing every single day scared me. I also wrote for *diaTribe*, a free once-monthly online patient resource (at the time) that we usually scrambled to finish on Friday evenings.

 Third, I started using a continuous glucose monitor ("**CGM**") in 2010, a transformative Bright Spot for living well with diabetes. Armed with a glucose reading every five minutes, I now had a powerful feedback loop to discover what worked for my diabetes and what didn't. My learning curve accelerated dramatically, and as I began to identify my own Bright Spots and Landmines, my BGs and quality of life improved dramatically.

Since 2013, I've written about my own diabetes tactics, learning, and mistakes in a *diaTribe* column, Adam's Corner. It's been some of the most gratifying work of my life, but I've also had a nagging feeling: far too many people are still struggling like I did. I wondered...

Can I compile my biggest discoveries into a single, actionable guide from which others might benefit?
Can I bring a little more light to the diabetes darkness?
And can I make it accessible to everyone who wants to learn?

The product of those questions is the book you are about to read, made available to you by The diaTribe Foundation – the nonprofit that publishes *diaTribe*.

HOLD UP!

What Counts As A Diabetes

I first encountered the idea of "Bright Spots" in the masterful book on behavior change, *Switch*, by Chip and Dan Heath.[1] It's radically different from what we typically do in diabetes: find problems and focus on what's going wrong.

 DIABETES BRIGHT SPOTS **are positive behaviors and choices I want to replicate as often as possible. They are the things *I'm doing right* that I should try to duplicate:** what helps keep my BGs in range, improves my mental state, and if repeated consistently, would improve my health and quality of life? Most of this book is focused on these Diabetes Bright Spots, such as eating fewer carbohydrates at meals (I aim for less than 30 grams), remembering why in-range BGs benefit me TODAY (I'm happier, more productive, in a better mood, and a kinder person to loved ones), walking after I eat, and getting at least seven hours of sleep.

 DIABETES LANDMINES **are the mistakes I make over and over again that drive my BG out of range, ruin my mood, or make life more difficult; I want to find ways to stumble on them less often.** I first wrote about Diabetes Landmines on *diaTribe* after I noticed something important: I tend to make the same mistakes *repeatedly*, such as overeating treats to correct low BGs; eating white bread and potatoes; and asking unproductive questions like "How is this possible?" or "Why am I so terrible at this?" Clarifying these Landmines upfront has helped me develop a plan of attack: What safeguards can I set up to avoid them? How can I build routines that reduce the chances of stumbling onto them?

It's easy to come up with a vague list of things I "should" and "should not" do, but Bright Spots and Landmines need to be *useful*. That means hitting three criteria:

1 **SPECIFIC AND ACTIONABLE** | **"Eat healthy" does not count** as a Food Bright Spot – it's too vague. "Fill half my plate with vegetables" is much clearer.

2 **REALISTIC AND SUSTAINABLE** | **"Not eating" does not count** as a Food Bright Spot either – it's impossible to sustain. "Eat slowly and stop before I'm 100% full" is more realistic.

3 **IN MY CONTROL AND CHANGEABLE** | **"Bad weather" is not an Exercise Landmine** – it's out of my control. On the other hand, "overeating after exercise" is a Landmine that is changeable – I can find ways to avoid it.

BRIGHT SPOTS ARE MORE IMPORTANT THAN LANDMINES, BUT WE DON'T PAY ATTENTION TO THEM

Bright Spots outnumber Landmines in this book by more than 2:1. That's intentional, because Bright Spots are so overlooked, so undervalued, and have had such a huge impact on me.

Many psychology books talk about the brain's survival instinct, which looks for things going wrong and zeroes in on problems. In diabetes, this inevitably leads to negative self-talk: "I screwed up," "I'm terrible at this," "I can't do anything right." It also leads to finger-wagging advice from others: "Don't do this," "Stop doing that," "You're unmotivated," "You just don't care," "You're lazy."

After my girlfriend and I adopted our dog, Sencha, I was surprised to hear only one piece of training advice from the shelter: use *positive* reinforcement to encourage good behaviors. In other words, focus on Bright Spots – what is the dog doing right that should be reinforced and encouraged? What a radically different approach from what we usually do in diabetes: focus too much on those negative Landmines.

Research from Dr. Barbara Fredrickson (author of *Positivity*) suggests that a ratio of 3 positive emotions for every 1 negative emotion is critical for human flourishing. 3:1! Focusing on Bright Spots is key for any of us to live well, and for me, they have redefined my daily journey with diabetes.[2]

This is not to say we should all live in a land of false positivity – sometimes the best way to improve is to look at what's not working and do less of it. Indeed, Dr. Fredrickson points out that a 3 positive to 0 negative emotion ratio is not in touch with reality – we all experience challenges. My approach has been to find and focus on Diabetes Bright Spots as much as possible, but not to ignore Landmines. This book is organized accordingly.

HOW TO IDENTIFY BRIGHT SPOTS AND LANDMINES

 Reflect and question:

I often try to ask myself, "Is this behavior a Bright Spot I want to encourage or a Landmine I want to avoid?" It also helps to review my day or week: What did I do well for my diabetes and how might I do that more often? The questions at the end of each chapter and the end of the book will help you identify your Bright Spots and Landmines.

② Check BG more frequently (if possible):

It's hard to know what works and what doesn't – particularly around meals and exercise – without knowing what my BG is and how it changes in response to different choices. Using a BG meter more frequently or wearing CGM helps find cause-and-effect relationships, and therefore, identify Bright Spots and Landmines.

> *"When I do _____, what happens to my BG?"*

I'm painfully aware and frustrated that not everyone has the resources to check their BG more often. This book does not assume most readers are on a CGM, and I know insurance companies still make it difficult to access enough BG strips. This is criminal, as more frequent glucose data truly saves lives. If this applies to you, read the tips in chapter one on getting more strips.

③ Ask loved ones and friends to observe me:

"When I have in-range BGs after a meal, what did I eat? What foods do I eat when my BG goes high after meals or when I become moody and grumpy? What stresses me out and what helps me relax? What happens on days when I'm super motivated and take care of my diabetes?" Explain the concept of Bright Spots and Landmines to loved ones – they can pick up a lot!

PLEASE KEEP IN MIND...

What works for me may not work for you. I'm sharing deeply personal experiences throughout this book – including my own glucose data – not to boast or to show I have all the answers. What I truly care about is helping people with diabetes live better, and this book shares my own Bright Spots and Landmines in case they are:

- Useful for you to try.
- Strategies that you can adapt.
- Seeds to get you thinking about your own ideas.

This book is written for type 1 and type 2 diabetes, though a small number of Bright Spots and Landmines only apply to insulin users. If you don't use insulin, feel free to skip these passages. There is a big focus on glucose monitoring throughout the book, since it's a key feedback mechanism for identifying Bright Spots and Landmines. Even if you don't currently monitor your glucose, I think many sections of this book will still benefit you.

Consult with a healthcare provider before making big changes to your routine, particularly if you do use insulin or medications that can cause hypoglycemia. Expert diabetes healthcare providers have reviewed this book's content (see the Gratitude section), but I am not a licensed medical professional.

I have been profoundly lucky throughout my diabetes journey, and this book is colored by that experience. My daily struggles are small compared to the heroic efforts of many people with diabetes. Far too many still lack access to even the most basic medications and devices, let alone to newer products. That is a travesty. This book cannot possibly solve the challenges of everyone, but my hope is at least one tip or question or quote may help you.

HOW TO MAKE THE MOST OUT OF THIS BOOK

Build incrementally and do not attempt huge leaps of change. Try adding or subtracting one or two things before moving on to more. This book should be seen as a toolbox of tactics I've found helpful, not a checklist of things to complete every day. You can always come back to your list or to the book if the change isn't working or if you've mastered it.

Feel free to skip to the chapter of the book you need the most: food, mindset, exercise, and sleep. I also encourage skipping around within each chapter. Everything in here has made a difference for me at some point, but I'm often struggling with one area the most. I've written this book so that each chapter can stand alone. The conclusion is useful even if you've only read part of the book.

Some Bright Spots and Landmines overlap. I've found that phrasing a specific insight in both a positive and negative context can help in different situations.

Try the questions at the end of each chapter – your answers will be more personal and valuable to you than anything I can write.

As I wrote this book, I tried to keep in mind your most precious resource: TIME. *Bright Spots & Landmines* is about half the length of a typical non-fiction book and contains only the most actionable tips that have made a difference for me. The four chapter summaries cover these in just one to two pages each.

I hope you can encourage your Bright Spots, avoid your Landmines, and live better with diabetes. Please write with feedback by emailing **brightspots@diatribe.org** – I would love to hear from you!

Onward!

ADAM BROWN
San Francisco, California | Spring 2017

01

Food

Eating for In-Range Blood Sugars and
Navigating a Tough Food Environment

CHAPTER SUMMARY

🍴 Food

MY BRIGHT SPOTS | p. 20

- Eat less than 30 grams of carbohydrates at one time
- Choose breakfast foods high in protein, fat, and fiber (e.g., chia pudding, eggs)
- Check BG 2–3 hours after meals (or wear CGM) to learn what foods work and make course corrections
- Fill half of my plate with vegetables
- Dose insulin 20 minutes before eating a meal with 30 grams of carbs or more
- Eat an early dinner more than three hours before bedtime, no snacking afterwards
- Cook at home instead of eating out
- In restaurants, order vegetables to replace normal side dishes
- Eat berries instead of traditional desserts
- Snack on nuts and seeds
- Ask: "Am I actually hungry, or am I just bored, tired, or near food?"
- Eat slowly and stop before I'm 100% full
- View food purchases like a political vote: what kind of organization am I supporting?

MY LANDMINES | p. 66

- Hypoglycemia binge: overeating to correct a low or using it as an excuse to "treat myself"
- White foods: bread, potatoes, rice, noodles, baked goods, crackers, chips, sugar
- Junk food in the house, snacks in sight, eating directly out of the package
- Packaged foods with more than 10 ingredients and high doses of sugar ("foodlike substances")
- Sugary drinks: fruit smoothies, big bottles of juice, regular soda, sweet tea, milkshakes, sports drinks
- Too many exceptions ("Just this once!") and excuses ("I earned it!")

QUESTIONS TO ASK YOURSELF | p. 82

MY FOOD BRIGHT SPOTS

 Eat less than 30 grams of carbohydrates at one time

Eating fewer carbohydrates at one time is the most important Bright Spot I've ever discovered for tackling the hardest part of diabetes: food. I aim for less than 30 grams of carbs at one time, and from many years doing it, I've experienced a slew of amazing benefits:

- Keeps my BG in the tight range of 4-8 mmol/l for 75% of the day or more.
- Brings a low average BG under 7 mmol/l, equating to an A1c of around 6%.
- Almost never causes extreme BG values less than 3 mmol/l or over 11 mmol/l (just 0.7% of the time).
- Uses 50%-80% less mealtime insulin than higher-carb meals, dramatically shrinking the risk of a dangerous insulin overdose.
- Requires less time thinking and worrying about diabetes.
- Eliminates lots of mood swings and mental fog, since my BGs are more predictable.
- Brings less hunger and hypoglycemia food binges.
- Keeps my weight, cholesterol, and blood pressure at goal.

Eating fewer carbs sounds "restrictive," but the game-changing diabetes and quality-of-life benefits have come from filling and tasty food (see my meal plan on page 25). I eat a lot of vegetables, nuts, seeds, olive oil, eggs, fish, chicken, beef, and some berries – typically about 70-120 grams of carbs per day (10%–15% of my daily calories), and most of those carbs come from fiber. The majority of my calories come from fat (60%-70%), with the rest from protein (15%-20%). This low-carb, high-fat approach works far better than the lame food advice I got after diagnosis.

I've found what works for me after reading the research, trying different eating approaches, learning from others with diabetes, and looking at my own glucose data and lab results. My most recent three months of continuous glucose monitoring (CGM) data, shown below, demonstrate the Bright Spot impact of eating fewer carbs: a steady average BG of around 6.5 mmol/l throughout the day (black line) and glucose values consistently in my goal range of 4-8 mmol/l (narrow gray bars). I've seen identical patterns for several years now, and while food choices are not the *only* factor responsible, they play a far bigger role than anything else. Plus, this eating approach requires *less* diabetes work!

This graph shows my data averaged over 90 days

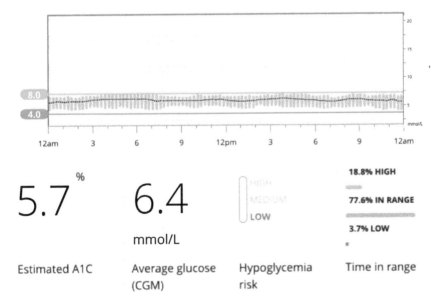

The BG benefits of eating fewer carbohydrates are not surprising: carbs raise BG far more than fat or protein, so limiting their intake has been a tremendous Bright Spot for reducing my highs and lows and cutting my insulin needs. Low-carb meals generally increase my blood sugar by a very predictable 0-2 mmol/l over a few hours, usually requiring just 0-2 units of insulin taken right when I start eating. Conversely, higher-carb meals can increase BG by 6-11 mmol/l within 30 minutes, need 2-10 times more insulin than low-carb meals, and require that insulin to be taken at least 20 minutes before eating.

Here's what the daily BG difference looks like, taken from my own low-carb versus high-carb experiments:

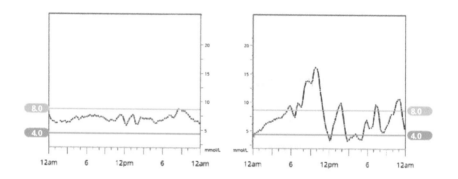

I find low-carb eating (left) is more like cruise control, giving predictable in-range blood sugars with less effort. I can put my diabetes in the background, since there is less need to carb count, less diabetes math to do, fewer swings in blood glucose, less medication to keep track of, less mental fog from highs and lows, and fewer worries.

Conversely, higher-carb eating (right) is like driving aggressively with the gas and brake, alternating between highs and lows – it's a scarier, rollercoaster drive that requires far more attention and diabetes effort.

I'm not a believer in "diets," which imply a short-term, exhausting sprint with a finish line. Eating is a big part of life, so it needs to be sustainable, enjoyable, and balance many factors: quality of life, diabetes hassle, glucose numbers, taste, weight, cholesterol, and more.

Eating fewer carbs is the single most important decision I've ever made for keeping my blood glucose in a tight range, taking insulin safely, reducing my diabetes burden and stress, and improving my quality of life and overall health.

This equation is different for every person, though many *diaTribe* readers with diabetes (including many parents) have written me with identical experiences. Some researchers agree too: a recent review in the journal *Nutrition* argued that reducing carbohydrates should be the "first approach" to managing type 2 diabetes and is "the most effective" addition to insulin in type 1 diabetes. The 26 authors reference 99 other publications to make their case.[3]

I certainly wish I could go back in time and give myself this Bright Spot food advice at diagnosis – it would have saved me ten years of out-of-control blood sugars and diabetes frustration.

IMPORTANT NOTES

Eating fewer carbohydrates can reduce insulin and medication needs; use caution to avoid hypoglycemia. Now that I'm adjusted to it, I actually experience less hypoglycemia with low-carb eating; since the insulin doses are so much smaller, my mistakes are also smaller and therefore less likely to result in lows. Work with a healthcare provider to reduce your medication doses safely.

Do not take my word for this! For the next week, try different amounts of carbs per meal – e.g., 15, 30, 60, and 90 grams – and monitor the impact on BG, mood, and energy levels over the next few hours. What patterns do you notice?

- **"Wait, how many grams of carbs are in _____?"** Everything in the **"What I Actually Eat"** section in the next pages has less than 30 grams of carbs in one serving, and most items have less than 15 grams of carbs. The best way to learn for yourself is to look at the grams of carbohydrates on nutrition facts labels on packages, use food apps like myfitnesspal and Lose It!, websites like **http://nutritiondata.self.com**, or simply search on Google with a phrase like "Carbs in raspberries." (In my experiments, Google answered pretty accurately, pulling data from a government database.) Pay careful attention to "serving size" – how large one portion is – since it drives the number of carbs. The beauty of choosing low-carb foods is that accurate carb counting becomes much less important.

Even eating just one low-carb meal per day can make a tremendous difference. I would choose breakfast if I only had to pick one, since it's usually the most challenging meal of the day with diabetes: high-carb and sugary options, little prep time, more insulin resistance, and often a high BG to begin with. (See the Bright Spot later in this chapter.)

Reduce carbs gradually and be patient – it takes at least two weeks for the body to adapt to lower-carb eating, according to researchers Drs. Jeff Volek and Stephen Phinney. Though you should see immediate BG results (in my experience), it can take time for the full range of benefits discussed above.[4] For more background, I highly recommend their book, *The Art & Science of Low Carbohydrate Living.*

A handful of healthcare providers and nutritionists I've met do not agree with this approach, arguing that not enough long-term research exists on low-carb eating. My own health data and quality of life has convinced me, without a doubt, that this is a critical Diabetes Bright Spot in the short- and long-term. Interestingly, eating more calories from fat and fewer from carbs has *improved* my cholesterol and triglyceride levels (lipids) and body weight, contrary to the typical advice about eating too much fat. Gary Taubes' excellent book *Good Calories, Bad Calories* or the shorter *Why We Get Fat and What to Do About It* delves into the fascinating and complicated connection between diet and heart disease.

BREAKFAST EXAMPLES

Chia seed pudding: ¼ cup chia seeds, ½ cup water (warm or cold) hearty amount of cinnamon, 1-2 tablespoons of coconut oil, topped with nuts, seeds, and frozen raspberries. Stir it for a minute, let it sit for a minute, then enjoy! Read more on this in the next Bright Spot.

Three-egg veggie scramble. For a more filling option, I add an avocado and a low-carb, high-fiber, whole wheat tortilla made by La Tortilla Factory. Each tortilla has 11 grams of carbs, with 8 of those grams from fiber, translating to little impact on BG.

- **"Nut/Seed Cereal"**: peanuts, almonds, sunflower seeds (shelled), and/or pumpkin seeds, topped with shredded coconut (unsweetened), cinnamon, and a splash of milk
- *Uncured* **turkey bacon** (no nitrates/nitrites added, except those naturally in salt and celery)
- **Almond flour or coconut flour baked goods:** pancakes, waffles, bread, or bagels (do not add sugar or honey)

LUNCH EXAMPLES

Giant salad with mixed greens, spinach, kale, or romaine; nuts or seeds; chicken, steak, or fish; parmesan cheese; dressing of choice (usually olive oil + red wine vinegar or Green Goddess)

Lentils with a bunch of veggies: ½ cup dry lentils, 1.5 cups water cooks a nice single serving

- **Snack foods (see page 29)** when I'm short on time, which seems to happen fairly often!
- **Egg scramble** with veggies
- **Roasted quarter chicken** with veggies
- **Turkey wrap** with a low-carb tortilla, veggies, slice of cheese and a side salad

- **Burger without the bun** (or a lettuce bun) with a side salad

DINNER EXAMPLES

Fajitas: sautéed chicken thighs, bell peppers, onions, guacamole, low-carb, high-fiber tortillas.

Half plate of vegetables plus a main course. See next page for some examples.

HALF A PLATE OF VEGETABLES

+

MAIN COURSE

- Broccoli
- Cauliflower
- Spinach
- Kale
- Bell peppers
- Asparagus
- Mushrooms
- Romaine lettuce
- Zucchini
- Brussels sprouts

SAMPLE COOKING METHODS

Sautéed on stove top with olive oil and garlic; steamed on the stove top or in the microwave; roasted in oven with olive oil, salt, and pepper; topped with a bit of parmesan cheese, soy sauce, or spices.

- Chicken thighs, breasts, or tenderloins (sautéed on stove top in olive oil or oven baked)
- Ground beef or turkey: stir fry, chili, burgers without the bun, meatballs (no bread crumbs or use almond flour)
- Steak
- Salmon
- Shrimp
- Calamari (no breading)

Cauliflower "rice" with veggies, scrambled eggs, soy sauce (great low-carb version of fried rice)

Almond flour crust pizza

- **Zucchini ("zoodle") pasta or lasagna**
- **Spaghetti squash** oven roasted and sautéed (pasta substitute)
- **Almond flour breaded chicken tenders**

SNACK EXAMPLES

- Peanuts, almonds, pecans, mixed nuts, macadamias
- Sunflower seeds (shelled), pumpkin seeds (in shell)
- Quesadilla with melted cheese in a low-carb tortilla
- Steamed vegetables with parmesan cheese or soy sauce
- Quest Bar protein bars (occasional treat; no sugar and 70% of the carbs are from fiber)

HYPOGLYCEMIA CORRECTIONS

(See the Food Landmine later in this chapter.)

- Glucose tablets
- Smarties
- Mini apples

DESSERT EXAMPLES

- Raspberries, strawberries, or blueberries (frozen or fresh; sugar should not be added)
- Small piece of 90% dark chocolate (occasional treat)
- Frozen mango chunks (occasional treat)

DRINK EXAMPLES

- Plain or sparkling water flavored with a fresh lemon or lime
- Loose leaf green tea (Japanese Sencha is my favorite)
- Black coffee
- Hot water with unsweetened dark chocolate cocoa powder (optional mint tea for a zero-sugar "mint chocolate chip" drink)

Choose breakfast foods high in protein, fat, and fiber (e.g., chia pudding, eggs)

My Bright Spot mornings start with a filling breakfast high in protein, fat, and fiber. That means a bowl of chia seed pudding, 2-3 scrambled eggs, nuts and seeds, uncured turkey bacon, or something made with almond flour (bread, pancakes).

Recently, I switched to chia seed pudding almost exclusively, a move I've called a "breakfast game-changer" in *diaTribe*⁵ (recipe on page 32). After sharing some of the advantages – little impact on BG, very filling and tasty, three minutes to make without cooking, inexpensive, and stocked with Omega 3s and fiber – I've been shocked at the positive response. Said one reader, "Adam, thank you so much. I've been looking for a breakfast like this for 25 years! It has changed my life."

Nailing breakfast sets the diabetes tone for the entire day, and options low in carbs and high in protein, fat, and fiber are a Bright Spot for several reasons:

 Very little BG increase (0-2 mmol/l) at a critical time of day. I'm more resistant to insulin in the morning and might be starting the day with a high BG anyways.⁶ The worst feeling is to wake up high and then go much higher, something these lower-carb options help avoid.

Chia seed pudding and eggs bring remarkably flat glucose profiles; these examples are typical of what I see about 90% of the time:

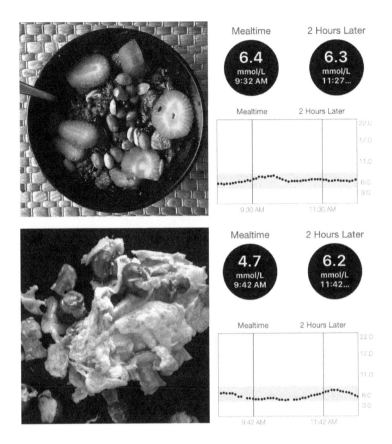

No need for an insulin head start. Low-carb, high-fat breakfasts usually allow for dosing insulin right as I start eating (or not at all), a huge advantage in the morning when time is of the essence. Most high-carb breakfast foods, by contrast, require taking insulin at least 20-40 minutes before eating to have any chance of managing the BG spike. (See the Bright Spot later in this chapter.)

Small doses of insulin (0-1 units for me), meaning I'm less likely to overshoot and crash low mid-morning when my productivity is highest, or when I'm walking into work.

Very fast to make. Chia seed pudding takes three minutes to make, requires no cooking, and is portable for traveling. Eggs take less than five minutes to cook.

5   **Keep me full for hours** and prevent overeating at lunch.

6   **Inexpensive:** eggs and chia seed pudding are less than $0.60 per meal.

Some of my loved ones might call my breakfast habits strange – "Chia seed pudding for breakfast? You're kidding, right?" But my perspective is a little different: "If it works for my BG, is fast to make, tasty, and improves my diabetes quality of life and daily hassle, why not?"

An absurd example of encouraging this breakfast Bright Spot comes from my study abroad in Hong Kong. I struggled with some of the carb-o-riffic breakfasts there and had to employ an unconventional but highly effective solution: buying eggs at the student grocery store, scrambling them in a bowl in my dorm, and cooking them in the microwave. This worked brilliantly, despite the funny looks I got from exchange students.

More recently, I've been known to mix chia seed pudding in Tupperware in the front row of a diabetes conference. When it comes to diabetes and food, my view is simple: effective beats unconventional!

WHAT HELPS ME

TO MAKE CHIA SEED PUDDING, I:

Mix ¼ cup of chia seeds, ½ cup of water, a hearty amount of cinnamon, 1-2 tbsp of coconut oil, and some combination of toppings like frozen raspberries, shelled sunflower seeds, and nuts. After about a minute of stirring with a spoon and about a minute sitting, it turns into a pudding-like gel. It can also be made in a batch ahead of time by quadrupling the recipe. The water can be hot or cold, depending on your preferences, and the pudding can be made thicker by using less water. Chocolate or vanilla protein powder or pure vanilla extract can be added for additional flavor. Parents have even emailed me with enthusiasm for this recipe – "My son loves this!" – meaning this isn't just a weird concoction for health nuts like me.

There is nothing "exact" about this recipe, so you can experiment with the components and toppings to fit your tastes. For example, I know someone that makes it with lemon juice, stevia, and almonds. There are other chia seed pudding recipes on the Internet, though most have way too much added sugar (including honey). **Important note:** If you have any GI discomfort with this recipe, make the chia pudding in a batch and let it sit overnight. Soaking chia seeds in water for a longer period of time has helped some readers who found my recipe hard to tolerate.

- **I generally take one unit of insulin for chia seed pudding,** which covers the very slow BG rise from fat, protein, and the small amount of carbs from the toppings. Each ¼ cup of chia seeds has 20 grams of carbs, though 16 grams are from fiber (80%), translating to little BG impact.

- **What on earth are chia seeds?** They look like poppy seeds and are packed with fiber, protein, and healthy Omega-3 fats. On their own, chia seeds don't taste like anything so it's all about how they are flavored (hence the recipe on the previous page).
- **I buy chia seeds in bulk online;** a two-pound bag from Viva Labs on Amazon costs about $10 and covers about 20 breakfasts. They can also be purchased at regular grocery stores and even corner stores, usually in one-pound bags.

BREAKFAST EGGS ARE A GREAT ALTERNATIVE TOO:

They increase glucose minimally, are filling, and help sneak in vegetables. The latest evidence suggests eggs do not raise blood cholesterol (the same is true for other sources of dietary cholesterol).[7] I often add a high-fiber, low-carb whole wheat tortilla and an avocado to make it a wrap that is even more filling[8], but has a minimal impact on BG.

TRY NON-TRADITIONAL BREAKFAST FOODS:

Almond or coconut flour to make pancakes and bagels; lentils; and even dinner leftovers. Who says breakfast has to be traditional? I think of it as just another meal.

ON A RELATED BREAKFAST NOTE, CAFFEINE CAN INCREASE BGS, AND I FIND THIS IS ESPECIALLY TRUE IN THE MORNING.

Several studies have found caffeine increases insulin resistance, stimulates the release of adrenaline, and can increase BG after consumption.[9] A big cup of coffee can easily increase my BG by 1-3 mmol/l, particularly in the morning when I'm more insulin resistant already. This is one reason why I drink green tea at breakfast – it has less caffeine and therefore a lower impact on BG.

If you find your post-breakfast BGs are consistently high, see if caffeine is contributing: try tea or stay off caffeine for a couple breakfasts. Some people I know actually take insulin to cover the BG increase from caffeine.

Check BG 2-3 hours after meals (or wear CGM) to learn what foods work and make course corrections

Driving a car with a completely blacked-out windshield would be dangerous - exactly the way I used to drive my diabetes when I didn't check my blood glucose very often. I had no idea where my BG was going, which made it difficult to stay in range.

Checking BG 2-3 hours after meals, or wearing a continuous glucose monitor (CGM), ensures I'm driving my diabetes safely and able to steer my blood glucose back onto the road (in range) if I'm going high or low. Plus, it provides useful meal feedback on what I did well or what I might do differently next time.

Course corrections: two meals with diabetes are rarely the same, and glucose data gives me actionable feedback to learn and correct mistakes quickly.

"My BG is very high (over 10 mmol/l); maybe I need some more insulin or could use a walk."

"I'm low (less than 4 mmol/l); I need to eat something."

"I'm in my target range (4-8 mmol/l); Nice! I'll try to do the same thing next time."

A BG check after eating ensures I won't ever stay out of range for too long after a meal.

Rapid feedback: What foods keep my BG in range? What foods are a challenge? Before getting on CGM, my breakfasts included granola bars, white bread and bagels, big bowls of cereal, and beyond. Since I wasn't checking my BG again until lunch, I had no idea that these foods were driving my blood sugar far out of range for hours at a time. More frequent glucose data after meals has made it easier to pair cause and effect and discover my Bright Spot and Landmine foods. CGM was actually a key reason for my move to lower-carb eating - the additional glucose data was like seeing my diabetes in a movie,

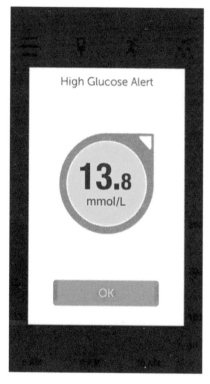

rather than isolated pictures (fingersticks) a few times per day.

Changing my mental reaction to post-meal blood sugar values has been critical for this Bright Spot: a 16 mmol/l or 2.9 mmol/l is not an indication of "failure" or a "bad grade"; it's a neutral data point to help me learn and change something right now. Chapter two discusses this in more detail, because it is so important and often forgotten.

WHAT HELPS ME

I aim to be in the range of 4-8 mmol/l within 2-3 hours after eating, using glucose data as my guide:

WEAR CGM IF IT'S ACCESSIBLE AND AFFORDABLE - THIS IS THE ONE DEVICE I WOULD RECOMMEND EVERY PERSON WITH DIABETES TRY OUT.

With a glucose reading every five minutes and a trend arrow, I always know what my blood sugar is, where it's going, and what different foods do - it's the ultimate Bright Spot and Landmine detection device! Plus, I can course-correct any out-of-range value with more confidence and safety. (I recognize not everyone can access these devices right now, but that should hopefully change in the coming years as new products come out.)

IF YOU CANNOT ACCESS YOUR OWN CGM OR DO NOT WANT TO WEAR ONE:

- **Take a fingerstick 2-3 hours after meals, and focus on doing this when BG is more likely to go out of range** - a high-carb meal, lots of activity, unfamiliar foods and restaurant meals, a large insulin dose, etc. It may help to focus on checking after a meal that happens at a consistent time each day - e.g., lunch at noon, BG check at 2 pm. Once the habit is built for that time of day, it's easier to expand to other meals. If you have access to very few strips per day, checking in pairs before and after a meal might require using more strips on some days and less on other days.
- **Ask your healthcare provider about "professional CGM."** These CGM devices are owned by the provider, placed at an office visit, and worn for a week or two at a time. Insurance often covers the cost.

Important safety note for course corrections: always account for "insulin on board" or "active insulin," meaning a bolus insulin dose taken in the past 3-4 hours that may still be lowering glucose.

"Stacking" too much new insulin on top of insulin on board ("IOB") can lead to low BGs. I generally assume about ⅔ of the insulin I took is gone after two hours - e.g., for a 3-unit bolus taken two hours ago, I would have 1 unit of insulin on board remaining. You may be different, and larger-sized boluses may hang around for much longer.

If you currently wear CGM, visit <u>diaTribe.org/CGMtips</u> for advice on getting better accuracy and making CGM a Bright Spot.

 **HOW TO GET MORE STRIPS**

PAY CASH AND BUY STRIPS OVER-THE-COUNTER OR ONLINE *OCCASIONALLY.* Visit **<u>diaTribe.org/getmorestrips</u>** for a list of accurate strip brands that have lower cash-pay prices. Sometimes, buying strips over-the-counter or online with cash can be less expensive (or similar) than using insurance.

IF YOU HAVE INSURANCE, USE "CO-PAY ASSISTANCE" PROGRAMS TO CUT THE COST OF STRIPS. These programs are sponsored by companies and can save you money when using insurance. You can often find these by searching for your strip brand and "co-pay assistance program." Visit **<u>diaTribe.org/getmorestrips</u>** for a partial list of co-pay offerings.

ASK YOUR HEALTHCARE PROVIDER FOR A LARGER STRIPS PRESCRIPTION - your co-pay will often remain the same.

Fill half of my plate with vegetables

When I fill half my plate with vegetables, I'm far more likely to have in-range blood sugars after a meal or snack. Why?

1 **Most veggies don't change BG very much, especially greens.** This chapter's first Bright Spot shares veggie examples with a small impact on BG, and the "cooking at home" Bright Spot has a shopping list. (The exception is "starchy vegetables" like potatoes, yams, corn, and beets, which can increase BG quite a bit; I avoid them.)

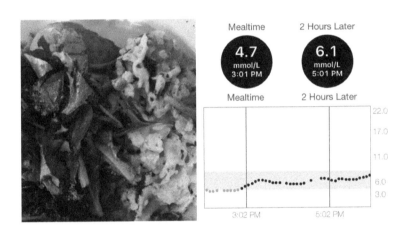

2 **Vegetables are super filling,** as they are packed with fiber and water and the perfect antidote to the constant hunger that often comes with diabetes. There is no better way to fill up than with a big plate of vegetables cooked in some olive oil.

3 **Eating vegetables leaves less room for Landmine Foods** that can really increase blood sugar, encourage overeating, and promote weight gain: dessert, fried foods, rice, pasta, white bread, sugary drinks, etc.

Despite these advantages, only 4% of Americans eat enough vegetables to meet the recommended levels: 2–3 cups per day. Additionally, average vegetable consumption has decreased 6% over the past five years.[10]

WHAT HELPS ME

FIND AN ENORMOUS SALAD I LOVE EATING AND CAN MAKE IN FIVE MINUTES AT HOME.

Mine is spinach, romaine, or kale; nuts and seeds; bell peppers and tomatoes; avocado or cheese; chicken, steak, or fish (optional); and whatever salad dressing I have around (olive oil + red wine vinegar, Green Goddess, etc.). I have a few huge salad bowls at home to ensure I really fill up on veggies.

- **It's very easy to make homemade salad dressing and save money on the bottles.** One I like to make uses ½ cup of red wine vinegar, 1 cup of extra virgin olive oil, 2 tbsp of Dijon mustard, ¼ tsp of salt, and ¼ tsp of pepper. This makes a great dressing for 4–6 big individual salads.[11]

HAVE A STOCKPILE OF FROZEN VEGETABLES IN THE FREEZER, WHICH REQUIRE JUST A FEW MINUTES TO STEAM IN THE MICROWAVE.

They won't spoil, are fairly inexpensive, and many experts say they are just as nutritious as buying fresh. I like broccoli with a little parmesan cheese or soy sauce on top. I usually steam frozen veggies in the microwave for a few minutes: place the veggies in a bowl, add a bit of water, and place a small dinner plate or microwave-safe cover on top.

USE VEGETABLES AS A SIDE DISH INSTEAD OF MORE TRADITIONAL SIDES LIKE RICE, PASTA, POTATOES, AND BREAD.

Even though potatoes are technically a "vegetable," I don't consider them one in this book – they increase BG pretty rapidly and come in the Landmine section of this chapter.

MAKE VEGETABLES IN NON-TRADITIONAL WAYS – zucchini noodles, spaghetti squash pasta, cauliflower rice, etc. Recipe books and websites have plenty of clever veggie ideas.

SIGN UP FOR A COMMUNITY SUPPORTED AGRICULTURE (CSA) PROGRAM.

These direct-from-farm services deliver amazing local produce at a great price. We use Imperfect Produce here in the San Francisco Bay Area and get a huge, customizable box of veggies for about $11-$15 each week. You can find more CSAs listed at **localharvest.org** (click "CSA").

 ## Dose insulin 20 minutes before eating a meal with 30 grams of carbs or more

When I do eat an occasional higher-carbohydrate meal (e.g., special occasion sushi meals), an insulin head start is critical for keeping my BG in range. Why? Most carbs raise blood sugar faster than the most popular rapid-acting insulins (Humalog, Novolog, Apidra) work. Here's what I've generally observed for myself, though these estimates vary by type of food and person:

	CARBS	RAPID-ACTING INSULIN (BOLUS/MEALTIME)
Begin Changing Glucose	↑ BG in 10 mins	↓ BG in 30 mins
Peak Effect	30-60 mins	60-90 mins

A 20-minute insulin head start can help with the lag time between carbs increasing BG and insulin dropping BG.[12] However, I need a longer head start when my BG is far above target (e.g., 14 mmol/l) or if I'm eating particularly "high glycemic" carbs that spike BG quickly (e.g., white rice). In those cases, I might need 40 minutes between taking my insulin dose and starting to eat!

This is one of the major reasons I also choose to eat fewer carbs - it takes out the annoying pain of an insulin head start, particularly at restaurants.

An exception to this Bright Spot is foods that contain lots of fiber, no sugar, and very few carbs (e.g., vegetables, nuts, seeds, beans, lentils), which usually don't need an insulin head start – the dose can be taken right as I start eating. I also skip the 20-minute insulin head start when my BG is less than 4 mmol/l going into the meal.

WHAT HELPS ME

TAKE MY INSULIN DOSE AND SET A 20-MINUTE COUNTDOWN TIMER ON A PHONE OR WATCH.

It prevents me from eating too soon, and also reminds me when to eat if I get distracted and forget.

WHEN BLOOD SUGAR IS HIGH, WAIT EVEN LONGER BETWEEN TAKING INSULIN AND EATING, OR take a short walk around the block before eating.

EAT SLOWLY AND CHOOSE FOODS THAT REQUIRE LESS OF AN INSULIN HEAD START: HIGHER IN FIBER, MORE FAT IN THE MEAL (e.g., olive oil, nuts, seeds, cheese), or lower in carbs. All these strategies can help delay or minimize the spike in glucose and give insulin time to catch up.

CHOOSE DIFFERENT OPTIONS AT RESTAURANTS, SINCE TIMING UNCERTAINTY CAN MAKE AN INSULIN HEAD START DIFFICULT.

I find it hard to have food served to me, take my insulin bolus, stare at the food for 20 minutes or more, and only then begin eating. What human can do this? The alternative is also challenging: accurately guessing exactly when food will be brought to the table, and then taking insulin at least 20 minutes before I expect it to arrive. Some of the restaurant ordering strategies I discuss later can minimize these challenges.

FOCUS ON AN INSULIN HEAD START AT THE MEAL I'M MOST LIKELY TO EAT AT THE SAME TIME EVERY DAY (USUALLY BREAKFAST).

This allows for a default time to take insulin: 7:40 am insulin dose before 8 am breakfast.

Eat an early dinner more than three hours before bedtime, no snacking afterwards

"Breakfast like a king, lunch like a prince, and dinner like a pauper."

MICHAEL POLLAN in *FOOD RULES*

When I eat a light, early dinner (6-7 pm) and do not snack afterwards, a wonderful cascade of Diabetes Bright Spots usually follows: my blood sugar stays in range all night, I sleep better, and I wake up in-range to start the day. It's remarkably effective. The picture below is a good example of what this looks like. I ate a big salad (greens, sunflower seeds, avocado, red pepper, olive oil and red wine vinegar dressing) more than three hours before bedtime, took a small amount of insulin, and didn't snack afterwards. My blood sugar stayed level for the entire night, a pattern I've seen repeatedly with this Bright Spot.

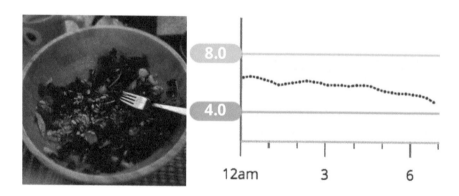

Conversely, eating a large dinner late at night or snacking right before going to bed usually looks like the below - I go from an in-range blood glucose around midnight (yay!) to a steady rise while I'm asleep. In this case, I pulled my classic Landmine: over-snacking on too many nuts and seeds before bed. (It would look much worse with high-carb snack foods like crackers.) I woke up at 5 am, took a correction dose, and then went very low around 8 am. As some of my friends with diabetes would say, "I took a ride on the GluCoaster!"

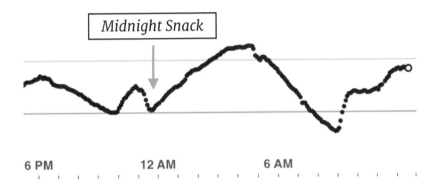

Midnight Snack

6 PM   12 AM   6 AM

WHAT HELPS ME

HAVE HALF A PLATE OF VEGETABLES, SOME PROTEIN (CHICKEN, FISH, BEEF), AND PLENTY OF FLUIDS AT DINNER (A BIG BOWL OF BROTH, A BIG GLASS OF WATER OR TEA).

The combo is filling enough that I won't feel hungry later (no pressure to snack), but light enough to keep my BG stable.

EAT MORE DURING THE DAY so I'm less likely to need a huge dinner.

FIND A BASAL* (BACKGROUND) INSULIN DOSE THAT KEEPS ME IN RANGE ON THIS EATING SCHEDULE OVERNIGHT.

Finding the right dose takes experimentation, and CGM has helped me enormously. I don't always get it right, but once I have a basal dose that keeps me level from bedtime to wakeup (within a 2 mmol/l range), I can stick to this schedule and know that I usually won't wake up low. The challenge, of course, is when I go off the schedule and eat a late dinner or snack, I will likely have high BG overnight. Routine definitely helps me here. Upcoming automated insulin delivery systems shine in this area, adapting to overnight needs by adjusting basal insulin based on CGM values every few minutes.

For those on injections, basal is the "long-acting" insulin dose, typically taken once or twice a day. For pumpers, this is the units/hour insulin delivery rate.

IMPORTANT NOTES

1 Be cautious if you exercise an unusually high amount one day or use N or R insulin (NPH, Regular) – eating a small snack before bed might help prevent overnight lows in these cases.

2 If you live in a part of the world where late dinners are common, this Bright Spot may be tough to implement. The best workaround is to find an insulin plan that fits your late-dinner schedule: covering the meal and holding BG steady overnight (within a 2 mmol/l range). A healthcare provider and CGM data can help optimize your dose.

 ## Cook at home instead of eating out

The food environment is a minefield for managing diabetes, and one of the easiest ways to beat it is cooking at home. I can control what's in the food, tailor it to my tastes, make sure I get enough vegetables, and save a lot of money. I also find cooking pretty fun, and it's been a terrific way to build awareness about what ingredients go into meals.

Restaurants are incentivized to give super economic value, to deliver great taste, or both. Those often translate into massive portions I feel obligated to finish ("I've got to get my money's worth"), food that comes covered in sugary sauces, menu items that drive my blood sugar way out of range (e.g., white bread, rice, potatoes), portions that are difficult to carb count, and more social temptation to eat Landmine foods.

Cooking at home means I don't have to battle these challenges, and it is 5-10 times cheaper than eating out. My shopping list (see page 50) averages out to only $1-3 per meal.

I didn't really cook when I was young, so it was a very new concept when I started living on my own. My roommate in college, a body builder, would shamelessly grill 10 chicken breasts at a time on the George Foreman Grill in our dorm. Shirtless! It didn't teach me gourmet cooking skills, but I sure learned how to cook a fine chicken breast and not feel absurd while doing it. (The volume of chicken grilling was so extensive that my other roommate's clothes started *smelling like chicken breast* with all-purpose meat seasoning. This did not go over well with his girlfriend.)

I'm not a frequent recipe cooker because I'm usually short on time and don't own the random ingredients they often call for. Recipes and cookbooks have been terrific for teaching me general principles and for the joy of cooking a new meal once or twice a week with my girlfriend. However, I have not been able to sustain frequent use. A basic rack of spices, olive oil, salt and pepper, a frying pan, and a stove-top can handle an astonishing array of great meals that take 20 minutes or less to make.

WHAT HELPS ME

HAVE A REPERTOIRE OF FAST, GO-TO RECIPES – sautéing vegetables with olive oil and garlic; scrambled eggs; sautéed salmon, chicken, beef, ground turkey with veggies; canned tuna or salmon or sardines on a salad; lentils and beans; etc.

MAKE A GROCERY RUN FOR EVERYTHING I NEED FOR A WEEK, and use online ordering to buy certain items in bulk (see list on page 50).

HAVE BACKUP FOOD THAT LASTS: frozen vegetables and fruit, canned food, peanut butter, etc. This ensures there is always something to eat at home when fresh supplies run low.

INVEST IN QUALITY NON-STICK PANS TO SAVE FRUSTRATION.

Purchasing a frying pan set made by T-fal has really improved my enjoyment of cooking – nothing is more frustrating than a sticky pan that ruins the food and my mood. Great non-stick frying pans are usually not too expensive (around $30-$40), and the time savings on cleaning alone is well worth the investment.

MAKE ENOUGH FOOD TO HAVE LEFTOVERS FOR MULTIPLE MEALS.

This can be a double-edged sword – more leftovers can lead to more food waste – so I try to eat leftovers really quickly. It's always a good reminder to look at some of the statistics on wasted food: an estimated 25%-40% of food grown, processed, and transported in the US alone will never be consumed![13] When I remember that, I do not let my leftovers go bad.

USE RECIPE BOOKS OR ONLINE BLOGS FOR NEW IDEAS, BUT DON'T FEEL COMPELLED TO COOK THEM EVERY DAY.

"Low carb," "paleo," "ketogenic," "gluten-free," and "vegetarian" cookbooks and websites have helped me find many great recipes, though the devil is always in the details; sometimes they still pack a lot of carbs in. I look for less than 15 grams of carbs in one serving, with most of those carbs from high-fiber sources like vegetables.

WATCH EXPERT CHEF AND COOKING VIDEOS ON YOUTUBE.

I always learn helpful tips and tricks from watching pros like Gordon Ramsey and Jamie Oliver.

SOME OF MY FRIENDS WITH DIABETES DON'T CONSIDER THEMSELVES "LOW-CARB," BUT HAVE BENEFITTED FROM A "GLUTEN-FREE" APPROACH that avoids traditional wheat products like pastas, breads, crackers, and other baked goods. For more information, see **http://celiac.org/live-gluten-free/glutenfree diet/food-options/**

A TYPICAL GROCERY LIST

I don't buy all the below each week, but the list reflects the foods I often eat over the course of several weeks. I typically shop at my local chain grocery store, but get some vegetables from a local corner market and a Community Supported Agriculture program. A few items are also much cheaper in bulk online.

VEGETABLES

- Salad base: spinach, kale, romaine, mixed greens
- Bell peppers
- Asparagus
- Broccoli
- Onions
- Squash
- Zucchini
- Mushrooms
- Garlic
- Green Beans

FRUIT

- Avocados
- Tomatoes
- Lemons and limes
- Strawberries
- Raspberries
- Blueberries
- Apples (small size)
- Mangoes (frozen) as an occasional treat

PROTEIN

- Eggs
- Chicken thighs, tenders, and breasts
- Steak and ground beef (grass fed is ideal, but it is more expensive)
- Ground turkey
- Salmon
- Tuna
- Shrimp
- Squid
- Canned sardines in olive oil
- Cheese: Mozzarella, parmesan, and cheddar

CONDIMENTS

- Salsa
- Sriracha
- Dijon mustard
- Parmesan cheese
- Soy sauce
- Salad dressing: olive oil and red wine vinegar (made at home), Green Goddess, Caesar

DRINKS

- Plain sparkling water
- Dark chocolate, unsweetened cocoa powder
- Loose leaf green tea
- Coffee

PANTRY

- Olive oil and coconut oil
- Chia seeds (Viva Labs or similar, purchased in two-pound bags on Amazon)
- Sunflower seeds (shelled) and pumpkin seeds (in shell)
- Peanuts, almonds, pecans, mixed nuts
- Almond flour and coconut flour (Bob's Red Mill or similar, purchased in a four-pound case on Amazon)
- Low-carb, high-fiber, whole wheat tortillas (La Tortilla Factory)
- Occasional canned beans (black, kidney, pinto) and dry lentils
- Occasional Quest Bar protein bars

In restaurants, order vegetables to replace normal side dishes

Counting carbs is difficult in restaurants, and knowing when the food is coming makes it hard to take insulin before the meal. I rely on one ordering strategy above all others: substitute vegetables in place of whatever default side dish is included. Usually it goes something like this:

> *"I'll take the salmon, but instead of potatoes, can I just get a side of vegetables?"*

> *"I'd like fajitas please, but no rice and no tortillas. Instead, I'll just have vegetables on the side."*

This approach is a beautiful way to change the environment and set myself up for making a Bright Spot choice. When the plate arrives, I don't need to exercise willpower to resist the side dish – it's simply not there to tempt me. This strategy also helps narrow the options when ordering from a big menu. I'm always looking for a main course entreé (e.g., meat, fish, eggs) that I can add a vegetable to, or a salad that looks appealing.

A MEAL I ATE AT AN AMUSEMENT PARK– proof you can often find something decent to eat, even in the heart of fast food.

Waiters and restaurants are happy to make this substitution, though a small fraction make me feel slightly awkward. One time in a Thai restaurant, the waiter was astonished that I didn't want a side dish of rice with my Chicken Ka Prow. My "special order" – yes, serving me *less food* - resulted in a yelling match in Thai across the restaurant with the chef. I assume it was something to the effect of, "This guy says he doesn't want rice. Can we even do that?" Other waiters will say things like, "What, no rice?! You don't like rice?!" But 99% of the time, they end up serving me exactly what I ask for anyways, bonus vegetables included. I always have to remember that "I'm the customer," and it's my diabetes at stake.

On the other hand, I always regret going with the standard order and planning to "just have a few" French fries or a "couple bites of rice" or a "sliver of the bread." Once I have one, the floodgates are open, and I can easily finish most of the plate. "Moderation" doesn't work for me at restaurants, which is why this ordering Bright Spot helps so much.

There are a few places where this strategy needs tweaking.

Burger and sandwich places: I'll order a burger and ask for no bun at all, or ask for it to be wrapped in lettuce. Dealing with high BGs and sluggishness from white bread is just not worth it. I usually eat sandwiches open-face (one slice of whole grain bread), and I always ask for a side salad instead of fries or chips.

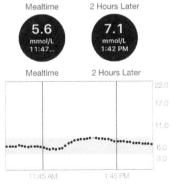

Mexican restaurants: I usually order fajitas with black beans and without any rice or tortillas. "Salad Bowls" are also a great option at restaurants like Chipotle, as you can avoid the rice and tortillas and just get beans, veggies, chicken or steak, guacamole or cheese, and salsa:

Otherwise, most of the core Mexican dishes have tons of carbs (tacos, burritos, enchiladas, rice, chips, etc.) that raise BG and are very difficult to bolus for correctly.

When an entire dish is based around pasta or rice: In those cases, I don't order it and find something else. A chicken or fish dish with a side of vegetables is almost always available.

Pizza restaurants: They often sell salads, but not always. I opt for chicken wings if they are not breaded (I always ask the waiter to clarify). This is where it helps to have supportive friends and loved ones, who are happy to go somewhere else. If you do have pizza on special occasions, try ordering the thinnest crust possible to minimize carbs.

WHAT HELPS ME

AUTO-PILOT ORDERING AT RESTAURANTS:

"I'll take _____ (meat, fish, eggs), but instead of the _____ (rice, pasta, bread, potatoes), can I have a side of vegetables?"

ORDER SALADS WHEN THE SIDE-DISH VEGETABLE SWAP IS NOT AN OPTION.

I ask for dressing on the side, no dried fruit like raisins, and no croutons, tortilla strips, or other carb-y crunches.

TELL THE WAITER NOT TO SERVE ME THE HIGH-CARB SIDE DISH OR BRING BREAD TO THE TABLE.

Often, I say "I won't eat it," just so they know it will definitely go to waste if they bring it. It's easier to have willpower when ordering than when the food is right in front of me.

"EAT DEFENSIVELY" - FILL UP ON VEGGIES OR OTHER LOWER-CARB OPTIONS AT *HOME* BEFORE A RESTAURANT MEAL.

One of my friends with diabetes uses this strategy frequently, and I love how it guards against challenging menus with no optimal choices. If I go into a restaurant meal 50%-75% full, I'm less likely to overeat or stumble on Food Landmines that drive my BG high.

Eat berries instead of traditional desserts

Traditional desserts – baked goods, cake, milkshakes, etc. – are usually a blood sugar nightmare. Unfortunately, the "sweet tooth" is sometimes difficult to ignore, particularly when everyone around me is eating dessert. Eating berries (strawberries, blueberries, raspberries) instead of typical desserts is my Bright Spot workaround: sweet enough, filling, not high in carbs, fairly easy to carb count, and unlikely to cause a major BG spike.

I always have frozen berries at home, which are cheaper than fresh options, just as tasty, easy to buy at most stores, and perfect for zero-hassle snacking when I'm not quite full after a meal. A local market near us also has great fresh strawberries that cost just a few dollars per pound.

Strawberries and raspberries are Bright Spot fruits because they are high in fiber and very low in sugar - combined, that brings a smaller BG increase. One cup of raspberries has just 15 grams of carbs, with 8 grams from fiber and only 5 grams from sugar. That's much better than pineapple or bananas, which have three times as much sugar and half as much fiber in one cup.

Often I will pair a berry dessert with a warm beverage I enjoy drinking after dinner. My go-to after dinner is what I call "chocolate drink" - one tablespoon of unsweetened dark chocolate cocoa powder mixed into hot water. It makes a rich and savory cup that I actually enjoy more than sweet desserts. Adding a peppermint tea bag turns it into a "mint chocolate chip drink," but without any increase in BG.

WHAT HELPS ME

STOCK UP ON FROZEN BERRIES and buy big bags in bulk to reduce the cost.

WHEN EATING OUT, ASK FOR A BOWL OF BERRIES INSTEAD OF AN ON-MENU TRADITIONAL DESSERT.

The more I practice it, the more I overcome the fear of asking for a "special" modification.

ADD FROZEN BERRIES OR SOME DARK CHOCOLATE CHIPS TO MY CHIA PUDDING AS A "SAVORY" DESSERT.

See the recipe in the breakfast Bright Spot.

FIND AN HERBAL TEA I LOVE DRINKING AS A DESSERT OPTION (PEPPERMINT, VANILLA ROOIBOS, ETC.).

The variety is truly endless, with many sweet- or savory-tasting options that don't add sugar or carbs.

DON'T HAVE TRADITIONAL LANDMINE DESSERTS IN THE HOUSE.

The more convenient they are to eat, the more likely I will eat them. Read more on this in the Landmines section of this chapter.

Snack on nuts and seeds

I eat more nuts and seeds than anyone I know. They work great as a snack on the go (gas stations and airports almost always have them), a fast breakfast, and even a light lunch when time is crunched.

Like other Bright Spot foods in this chapter, nuts and seeds bring a consistent and pretty flat BG pattern: a slow rise of 0-2 mmol/l over a period of a few hours. Unless I'm eating a huge quantity at one time, I usually don't take any insulin at all. These patterns for almonds and peanuts are typical of what I see 95% of the time:

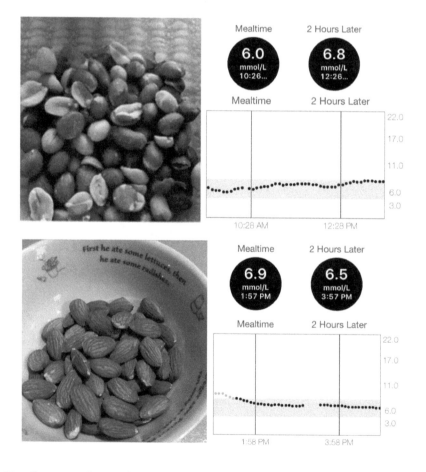

(Sunflower and pumpkin seeds and most nuts are pretty similar.)

Nuts and seeds are packed with fiber and healthy fats, which makes them filling and stops hunger in its tracks. I also love that they don't require cooking. Like all snacks, of course, this one is very easy to overeat. I always try to pour them into a bowl first, buy unsalted options in smaller packs, and avoid them after dinner.

BUY NUTS AND SEEDS IN THE BULK SECTION OF THE STORE OR ONLINE TO SAVE MONEY.

I often stock up on peanuts and sunflower seeds (shelled), since they go well with my chia seed pudding and are much less expensive than almonds and mixed nuts.

DON'T EAT TOO MANY CASHEWS, as they have more carbs and less fiber than other nuts.

STEER CLEAR OF NUTS AND SEEDS THAT ARE "CANDIED" OR HAVE ADDED "SUGAR," "HONEY," AND UNRECOGNIZABLE INGREDIENTS.

I'll only buy a package of nuts and seeds if the only other ingredients are oil and salt.

MAKE A NUT-SEED HOMEMADE "CEREAL" AS A SNACK:

Peanuts, almonds, sunflower seeds, and/or pumpkin seeds, topped with shredded coconut (unsweetened) and cinnamon. Milk is optional, but does give it a nice "cereal" feel.

Ask: "Am I actually hungry, or am I just bored, tired, or near food?"

I love food like anyone else, but too often, my brain wants something to eat when I don't even need it – especially in a food environment where snacks and restaurants and advertisements are everywhere! When I aimlessly wander into the kitchen at 10 pm or an hour after lunch, one Bright Spot question often helps:

Most of the time, I'm NOT actually hungry, but simply smelling or noticing nearby food, procrastinating, or feeling sluggish. The question reminder helps me realize it.

The obvious exception is when I'm low (and often very hungry), in which case I try to eat glucose tabs, Smarties, or a single piece of fruit – quantity limited is key. As I'll discuss in the Landmines part of this chapter, using lows as an excuse to overeat is something I always regret.

WHAT HELPS ME

WHEN DESIRING A SNACK, DRINK WATER OR PLAIN TEA (UNSWEETENED) FIRST; I'M OFTEN MISTAKING HUNGER FOR THIRST.

I carry around a large reusable water bottle, and have lots of loose leaf green tea at home and at work. (It's far tastier than bagged tea, and I buy it online and make it in a French press.) Half of a water bottle or a few cups of tea works wonders for quenching my appetite between meals.

SET BLACK-AND-WHITE RULES TO PREVENT MYSELF FROM SNACKING INDISCRIMINATELY JUST BECAUSE FOOD IS AROUND:

"No food after dinner" (unless I am low).

"At least three hours must pass between snacks or meals" (unless I am low).

BUILD AWARENESS BY TAKING PICTURES OF MEALS OR USING A LOGGING APP FROM TIME TO TIME.

It's hard to know how much and how often I'm eating unless I actually measure it. Pictures are fast and easy, and a growing number of apps like mySugr can now overlay photos with BG data. But I've found even just tracking my meals for a week with a food app, a handwritten notebook, or simply taking smartphone photos works wonders for bringing more awareness to what I'm consuming and the impact on BGs.

 Eat slowly and stop before I'm 100% full

Eating slowly and stopping before I'm 100% full are remarkably effective at preventing two of my biggest food traps: eating too quickly and overeating.

I often feel guilty for overeating, but interestingly, people with diabetes are more apt to overeat for at least two reasons:

1 We are either missing or have lower levels of hormones like amylin that suppress appetite.[14] This is rarely discussed and so important - it makes self-control around food much harder with diabetes.

2 Both high and low BGs can cause hunger, particularly lows.

It can take 15-20 minutes after food is first eaten for the range of fullness (satiety) signals to reach the brain.[15] Boy, is it easy to overeat in that time frame!

I use many different tips for eating slower and stopping before I'm exploding (see below), and the most useful options operate on auto-pilot and don't require memory or self control - for instance, using smaller dinner plates, eating huge salads or lots of veggies, and drinking plenty of water or tea.

WHAT HELPS ME

USE SMALLER PLATES. Studies repeatedly show this is an effective environment trick to eat less. I find 8-inch dinner plates are the perfect size. Read *Mindless Eating* by Dr. Brian Wansink or visit the Cornell Food & Brand Lab site at **foodpsychology. cornell.edu**.

The same amount of food on a smaller plate looks more filling.

FILL UP ON GREEN VEGGIES (HALF MY PLATE), HAVE A HUGE SALAD, AND GO FOR VEGGIE SECONDS FIRST.

As noted earlier in the chapter, aiming for half of each plate with veggies provides a great and easy to remember visual.

EAT SLOWER THAN THE PEOPLE I'M EATING WITH.

With at least one other person across from me, it's easy to see how relatively fast I'm finishing my food, and to adjust so I'm less speedy.

DRINK AMPLE WATER OR TEA AT MEALS (16 OUNCES), OR HAVE A LARGE BOWL OF BROTH SOUP BEFORE EATING.

This is an area where bigger is better – the larger the cup or bowl, the more liquid I will consume.

SERVE FOOD IN THE KITCHEN, EAT AT THE TABLE, and go back for seconds only after 20 minutes have passed and I still feel hungry.

USE CHOPSTICKS OR PUT MY FORK DOWN BETWEEN BITES.

These strategies dramatically slow down my usual fast pace of eating.

REMIND MYSELF THAT I DON'T HAVE TO CLEAN MY PLATE.

This cultural relic is tough to overcome with diabetes, but I can always pack my meal up and save it for later. Yes, the first bite is good, but the 26th bite is usually unnecessary. Loved ones can help too with just a simple nudge: "Honey, you don't have to finish it."

View food purchases like a political vote: what kind of organization am I supporting?

Fast food is tasty, cheap, and convenient – a persuasive trifecta! Unfortunately, I always regret eating it: the added sugar, white bread, and French fries are horrible for managing blood sugars and very difficult to carb count.

One of my Bright Spots for avoiding fast food is to mentally reframe the purchase decision: every dollar I spend at McBurgerTown is a vote of support in favor of these institutions and what they stand for. Do their foods advance my health and make me feel great? Do I support their food and advertising practices? Would I want my picture on the front page of a newspaper next to their logo?

No, no, and no.

This mindset sounds radical, but when I'm in the airport weighing between a personal pizza and fries versus a salad, or in the grocery store choosing between a frozen burrito versus fresh vegetables and chicken, the decision is usually automatic – "I'm voting for my diabetes."

Plus, the more automatic decision-making criteria I have, the less likely I am to stumble onto Landmines.

WHAT HELPS ME

ASK, "IF I ATE FOOD FROM THIS ORGANIZATION EVERY DAY FOR THE NEXT 10 YEARS, would it have a positive or negative impact on my diabetes? Would it support the things I want to do in life?"

ASK, "WILL THIS DIABETES LANDMINE BE WORTH HOURS OF OUT-OF-RANGE BGS?"

Tasty food feels good, while high BGs do not.

WATCH DOCUMENTARIES LIKE *FOOD INC.*, *FED UP*, *SUPER SIZE ME*, AND RELATED FILMS.

These movies touch upon some of these themes and remind me that I "vote" with my dollar every single day.

MY FOOD LANDMINES

 Hypoglycemia binge: overeating to correct a low or using it as an excuse to "treat myself"

I consider myself someone with a lot of willpower, but with a blood sugar of 3 mmol/l, I just want to eat everything in sight. This leads to one of my biggest Landmines: overcorrecting a low blood glucose with too many carbs, only to go far too high afterwards.

The picture below is a real example of what I mean – that 14.7 mmol/l misfortune (265 mg/dl) occurred after I stormed the fridge at 2 am and corrected a nighttime low using free granola from a friend's work event. The huge bowl was sitting in our fridge, looked really good, and "I only had a little." DOH!

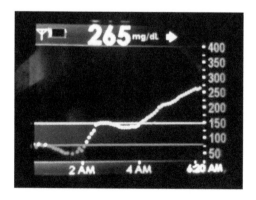

I've used four strategies to get around this trap, which are all directed at reducing bad impulsive decisions in the moment:

1 **Have go-to automatic corrections for hypoglycemia that are quantity limited and unappealing to overeat.** Glucose tablets and Smarties are predictable, relieve my low symptoms very quickly, and I know I won't overeat them. Some of my friends with diabetes count out jelly beans, 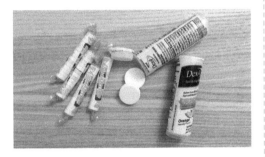 mini Swedish Fish, gummies, or hard candy - again, allowing them to modify the amount to match exactly what their BG needs.

2 **Fill in the blanks:**

Eating ___ (amount) of ___ (food) raises my BG by ___ mmol/l.
Example: Eating <u>one glucose tab</u> raises my BG by 1 mmol/l.

The only way to discover this is by checking BG, eating a food that has been measured out, and then checking again in roughly 15-30 minutes.

Knowing this helps me adjust the amount of food to raise BG to my target of 5.5 mmol/l, but not overshoot. Instead of a hypoglycemia binge, it's more of a precision dose of carbs. If I'm at 3.5 mmol/l, I know I need only two glucose tabs to get back to 5.5 mmol/l. If I'm exercising (including walking), have taken bolus insulin within the last three hours ("insulin on board"), or have a down-trending arrow on my CGM, I might add more carbs - glucose will continue to fall, so I need additional buffer.

3 **Do NOT use hypoglycemia as a justification to eat junk. Period.** It's enjoyable and easy to view a low as "treat time," but I always regret doing so. Plus, it connects a food reward (treat) with something I want to avoid (going low), an easy way to build a bad habit.

4 **CGM often has lag time in hypoglycemia; it should not be the only indicator of "I've recovered" or "I'm still low and need to eat more."** Continuing to see 3.3 mmol/l on my CGM encourages overeating correction foods, but often, my BG has recovered (5.5 mmol/l) and the sensor hasn't picked it up yet. If I still feel low and want to eat more, I try to confirm a CGM reading 10-20 minutes later with a glucose meter before eating extra correction carbs.

 White foods: bread, potatoes, rice, noodles, baked goods, crackers, chips, sugar

One of the great ironies of my job is that managing diabetes is *harder* at most conferences - places where the precise goal is to help people with diabetes do better! These are actual pictures I've taken at medical gatherings all over the world, where professionals and researchers are served BG Landmines with regularity:

I've become so frustrated with the state of affairs that I even call out conferences on Twitter:

#CONFERENCEFOODFAIL

Eating any of these foods results in a near-immediate spike in BG, followed by a wave of regret and sluggishness that takes hours to recover from.

A white food (inside or out) is one helpful marker for identifying some of these Landmines: white bread, potatoes (including French fries), rice, noodles, crackers, chips, and sugar. Brownish-looking baked goods, of course, are also made with white ingredients like sugar and flour.

These foods may be tasty and cheap, but in addition to spiking my BG very rapidly, white foods...

...ARE NOT FILLING AND EASY TO OVEREAT. | Consuming half a loaf of French bread or a few large cookies is easy when the food doesn't fill me up.

...REQUIRE LARGE DOSES OF INSULIN TAKEN LONG BEFORE EATING THEM. | A big dose of insulin increases the likelihood of a low BG, followed by a high BG from overeating the correction (a no-fun rollercoaster). Plus, I find insulin must be taken 20-40 minutes before eating these carb-loaded, sugary Landmines; otherwise, I have little chance of staying in range.

...ARE DIFFICULT TO CARB COUNT ACCURATELY. | It's tough to look at a plate and know exactly how many carbs are in a pile of rice or potatoes or a chunk of bread. Precisely measuring food out is a pain and is not always possible. Apps can be helpful, but still require accurately gauging portion sizes: Is this half a cup of rice? Is it 4 oz of chips?

... ARE NOT NUTRITIOUS and chemicals have often been added to preserve shelf life or amplify the taste.

WHAT HELPS ME

SUBSTITUTION is the easiest way to avoid this Landmine:

- **Rely on vegetables as my core side dish, making clever swaps:** zucchini or spaghetti squash can stand in for pasta, and blended cauliflower can substitute for rice (also sold pre-blended at some stores like Trader Joe's).

- **Eat berries** instead of traditional desserts.
- **Use almond flour or coconut flour as a substitute for baked goods, bread, and pizza crust.** These flours have a lower impact on BG, since they have 3–4 times fewer carbs and more fiber than traditional flours. For example, ¼ cup of almond flour from Bob's Red Mill has 6 grams of carbs (50% from fiber), while ¼ cup of white flour has 25 grams of carbs (only 4% from fiber).[16] Whole wheat flour does have slightly more fiber than white flour, but it has just as many carbs; that's why I recommend almond or coconut flour.
- **Buy low-carb, high-fiber tortillas as a bread substitute.** On the nutrition facts label, the grams of fiber should be very close to the grams of carbohydrate (e.g., 8 grams of fiber, 11 grams of total carbs).

REMEMBER HOW MUCH I REGRETTED EATING THE LANDMINE FOOD LAST TIME.

Often this is enough of a reminder to keep me away.

IN RESTAURANTS THAT SERVE FREE BREAD OR CHIPS:

- Tell the waiter, "No thanks, I won't have any. Please take them away."
- Put the bread or chips on the other side of the table next to someone else (out of my reach).
- Ask friends or family to "save me from myself" – "Please don't let me eat any of the chips." I'll have more to say about relying on loved ones in the Mindset chapter.

IF I DO EAT WHITE FOODS, WALK IMMEDIATELY AFTER EATING them to blunt the BG impact.

Junk food in the house, snacks in sight, eating directly out of the package

When I succumb to Landmine foods, or even when I overeat healthier snack foods, one of three situational factors usually plays a role:

- **The junk food was readily accessible in the house.** Since Landmine foods like crackers, chips, and sugary treats require no prep time, they are easy to reach for at night (tired, stressed) or when low, and are a go-to when I'm craving something sweet or salty but don't want to cook real food. "I'll just have a bite" and then I finish the package.

- **Food was in visible sight.** It's amazing how putting something on the kitchen counter or table - instead of hidden in a cabinet on a high shelf - dramatically increases my consumption. This can work in my favor (a bowl of berries on the table), but usually works against me (a see-through bag of tortilla chips on the kitchen counter). "I'll just have a few," and before I know it, I've eaten 40 chips one-by-one and am facing a high BG for hours.

- **I poured food directly from the package to my hand - repeatedly.** Overeating is pretty much guaranteed when I'm mindlessly reaching into the package, grabbing food, chomping it down, and going back for more. This happens often when my BG is low and I overeat food that won't relieve my low quickly: salty peanuts and peanut butter, sunflower seeds and mixed nuts, etc.

WHAT HELPS ME

KEEP JUNK FOOD OUT OF THE HOUSE COMPLETELY, OR AT MINIMUM, BUY IT LESS OFTEN.

If it's not around, I cannot eat it.

MAKE LANDMINE FOODS HARDER TO ACCESS AND LESS VISIBLE AT HOME:

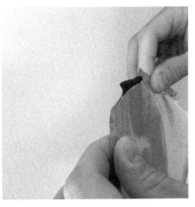

Top shelf of the pantry, smaller hole in the bag so pouring is more difficult, and rolled up tight with a bag clip. These strategies are effective at cutting my consumption – it takes more effort, time, and patience to access snacks. If junk food is in the house, the least I can do is never put it in plain sight and put up barriers to accessing it.

ALWAYS POUR SNACKS INTO A SMALL BOWL INSTEAD OF DIRECTLY INTO MY HAND, and use a smaller spoon to eat them (if applicable).

WHEN I'M HOME, STATION MYSELF AWAY FROM THE KITCHEN AND PANTRY – much of my snacking comes from being in the same room as food.

FIND A LANDMINE FOOD SUBSTITUTE THAT HAS A SMALLER BG IMPACT – bell peppers instead of chips for guacamole, salty nuts and seeds instead of crackers, frozen berries instead of candy, etc.

HAVE 16 OZ OF WATER, TEA, OR BROTH BEFORE I SNACK ON ANYTHING.

Often, just filling my stomach with fluid solves my snack cravings.

 ## Packaged foods with more than 10 ingredients and high doses of sugar ("foodlike substances")

Another good sign of a Diabetes Landmine is a packaged food with a long ingredient list (more than 10 items), usually filled with strange things like partially hydrogenated vegetable oil, high fructose corn syrup, Yellow #5, BHA/BHT, etc. These foods often have a hidden form of sugar listed in the first few ingredients, making them far more likely to drive my blood sugar out of range.

Author Michael Pollan calls these "edible foodlike substances" or "processed foods," and they are typically found in the middle aisles of the grocery store, are ultra-cheap, and frequently use misleading "healthy" marketing claims like "All Natural," "Low Calorie," etc.[17] These messages imply products like flavored yogurt, granola, and "energy bars" are great options, especially when they include gentle grassy fields on the label. The reality of long-ingredient-list foods is they are usually serious Landmines that increase blood sugar quickly and are not very filling.

For example, one popular breakfast pastry with 34 ingredients prominently features fresh blueberries on the box and is "Cholesterol Free," "Made with Real Fruit," and "A Good Source of Vitamins."

But this is a Diabetes Landmine if I've ever seen one: 38 grams of carbs per serving, nearly 50% of which are from sugar. Three out of the first four ingredients are another word for sugar: enriched wheat flour, *corn syrup, high-fructose corn syrup, dextrose*. Plus, these pastries generally come packaged in two-packs, so a single serving is really 76 grams of carbs and 32 grams of sugar.

Nutrition Facts	
Serving Size	1 Pastry (52g)
Servings Per Container	8

Amount Per Serving	
Calories 200	Calories from Fat 45

	% Daily Value*
Total Fat 5g	**8%**
Saturated Fat 1.5g	**8%**
Trans Fat 0g	
Cholesterol 0mg	**0%**
Sodium 170mg	**7%**
Total Carbohydrate 38g	**13%**
Dietary Fiber less than 1g	**3%**
Sugars 16g	
Protein 2g	

I used to eat foods like this all the time after I was first diagnosed. I don't anymore! But the average diet is filled with them: a recent study found that "ultra-processed" foods comprise a shocking 58% of the American diet, and more concerning for people with diabetes, contribute 90% of added sugar.[18] When I get those two numbers as low as possible, I see much better BGs with less medication and frustration.

WHAT HELPS ME

EAT WHOLE, SINGLE-INGREDIENT FOODS:

The less processed and packaged a food is, the better the impact on my BG.

CHECK INGREDIENT LISTS BEFORE BUYING FOODS. A SHORT LIST IS GENERALLY A GOOD SIGN (IDEALLY 1-5 ITEMS), WHILE A LONG LIST (MORE THAN 10 ITEMS) IS A RED FLAG.

This approach is unfortunately not perfect - e.g., a one-lb. bag of sugar has only one ingredient. Still, it's a good starting point.

WHEN SHOPPING, LIMIT FOODS FROM THE CENTER AISLES OF THE GROCERY STORE, where most of these packaged foodlike substances live. I stock up on the fresh, single-ingredient foods around the perimeter.

AVOID ANYTHING WITH MORE THAN 10 GRAMS OF SUGAR (WHOLE FRUIT IS AN EXCEPTION AND BERRIES ARE IDEAL).

Limiting sugar as much as possible has been a major Bright Spot for improving my BGs. As noted earlier, berries are ideal because they have less sugar and carbs than most other fruits.

KNOW THE MOST COMMON SYNONYMS FOR SUGAR AND AVOID FOODS THAT HAVE THEM, ESPECIALLY IF THEY ARE IN THE FIRST FIVE INGREDIENTS: sucrose, glucose, fructose, high-fructose corn syrup, corn syrup, dextrose, maltodextrin, fruit juice, fruit juice concentrate, brown rice syrup, maltose, honey, barley malt, coconut sugar, agave nectar.

AVOID ANY FOOD WITH "PARTIALLY HYDROGENATED" OR "HYDROGENATED" OILS.

Partially hydrogenated oils are another word for "trans fats," which are put into processed foods to make them last longer and taste better. They are harmful to the human body, increasing the risk of developing heart disease and stroke.[19] (This is in contrast to fats like nuts, seeds, and olive oil, which are generally associated with less risk of heart disease.[20]) Products can still be listed as "0 grams of trans fats" even if they contain 0–0.5 grams per serving - the only way to identify these foods is to look for "partially hydrogenated" oils in the ingredient list. To make things more complicated, some foods will only list "hydrogenated oils" as an ingredient, but contain a mix of the dangerous "partially hydrogenated" oils and the less controversial "fully hydrogenated" oils. UC Berkeley Wellness sums the ultimate point up well: "All this is more reason to limit or avoid foods that contain any type of hydrogenated oil. These foods - often baked sweets and snack foods - tend not to be healthy choices anyway."[21]

 Sugary drinks: fruit smoothies, big bottles of juice, regular soda, sweet tea, milkshakes, sports drinks

There is no faster way to spike my BG than with sugary drinks: fruit smoothies and bottles of juice, regular soda, sweet tea, dessert-like coffee drinks, milkshakes, and beyond.

Fruit drinks really frustrate me, because they give the "aura of health," but aren't much different from BG Landmines like regular soda. These "100% Juice" drinks often look nutritious (green plants!) and are even labeled "No sugar added," suggesting they are not a bad option. One commonly sold beverage (pictured) has 53 grams of sugar (!) from fruit in one serving, meaning it's allowed to say "No sugar added" on the bottle. There is also zero fiber or fat to blunt the spike in glucose. This is a BG Rocket Ship in a bottle, even if the product looks and sounds healthy.

Nutrition Facts

Serving Size 15.2 fl oz (450 mL)
Servings Per Container 1

Amount Per Serving

Calories 270	Calories from Fat 0

	% Daily Value*
Total Fat 0g	**0%**
Saturated Fat 0g	**0%**
Trans Fat 0g	
Cholesterol 0mg	**0%**
Sodium 25mg	**1%**
Total Carbohydrate 63g	**21%**
Dietary Fiber 0g	**0%**
Sugars 53g	
Protein 4g	

When I ask healthcare providers what advice they give to people with diabetes, this one almost always comes up: "Do not drink liquid carbs!" Small amounts of juice are of course useful for correcting hypoglycemia, but I find over-consuming juice is too easy - especially when it's packaged in a single-serving 15 oz bottle with 63 grams of carbs. Drinking just 2 oz of a juice smoothie when I'm low is just not going to happen, which is why I try to avoid sugary drinks at all costs.

(Caveat: Many of my friends with diabetes are fans of mini boxes like Juicy Juice for correcting lows, which are quantity limited and can overcome this trap.)

WHAT HELPS ME

DRINK PLAIN OR SPARKLING WATER OR UNSWEETENED TEA OR COFFEE.

I often use a lemon or lime in water to enhance the taste. It's nearly as good as drinking lemon-lime soda, and it comes in handy in a bar instead of drinking alcohol.

CHECK THE INGREDIENT LABEL FOR "0 GRAMS OF SUGAR" before drinking any bottled or canned beverage.

VIEW SUGARY DRINKS AS NO DIFFERENT FROM CIGARETTES: POISONING MY BODY AND POSSIBLY BUILDING A SUBSTANCE ADDICTION.

Some animal studies even suggest sugar affects the brain similarly to addictive drugs like cocaine.[22] Gary Taubes' newest book, *The Case Against Sugar*, covers this topic in more depth.

I STOPPED DRINKING DIET SODA AS A SUBSTITUTE ABOUT SIX YEARS AGO - IT HABITUATED ME TO CRAVING SWEET THINGS, WHICH IN TURN MADE ME MORE LIKELY TO EAT AND DRINK BG LANDMINES.

In the past few years, a handful of animal studies and at least one human study have suggested that artificial sweeteners can change gut bacteria, blood glucose, and hormones in negative ways.[23] Though the research is still very early, I go by the precautionary principle: diet soda won't improve my health and may even cause some harm.

 Too many exceptions ("Just this once!") and excuses ("I earned it!")

Exceptions are easy to make in the moment, but added up consistently over time, can amount to a pattern of Landmines. The challenge with exceptions is balancing:

The spontaneity and joy of allowing them (e.g., special occasions, "I earned it")

VS.

Deliberately trying to encourage my Bright Spots and avoid my Landmines.

These usually oppose each other, which means there is no perfect or one-size-fits-all solution. I'm the type of person that does not do well with moderation, meaning it's easier to make very few exceptions. Otherwise, an inch becomes a mile, and before I know it, I'm off track. It was hard at first to turn down desserts and high-carb meals and snacks, but once I committed to not eating them, it became automatic. Six years later, I don't think twice.

Part of this meant changing my identity:

Q: **What type of person am I?**

A: I'm the type of person that takes care of my diabetes and health. I'm the type of person that wants to think well, have energy to live life, and treat others well, meaning I need to spend more time in my target BG range (4-8 mmol/l).

Q: **How would a person like me behave in this scenario?**

A: I wouldn't eat these things!

I've internalized this self-assessment, and I've also tried to make it very clear with my family, friends, and coworkers: it brings social pressure to act in accordance with the idealized version of myself.

WHAT HELPS ME

SET GROUND RULES FOR MY EXCEPTIONS AHEAD OF TIME – OTHERWISE, IT'S EASY TO FALL INTO THE TRAP, "JUST THIS ONE TIME."

For example, I break my low-carb and no-white-rice goals about once per month when eating sushi, one of my favorite foods. I always take insulin at least 20-40 minutes before eating sushi and try to walk after these meals to minimize the impact of spiking my BG with white rice. (If my BG is over 8 mmol/l before eating sushi, I limit the amount I eat or choose sashimi and avoid the rice altogether.)

CLARIFY MY BRIGHT SPOTS AND LANDMINES AHEAD OF TIME, so I always have a guide to follow at meals.

QUESTIONS TO ASK YOURSELF

 ## Bright Spot Questions

Think about times when you see in-range blood sugars (4-8 mmol/l) 2-3 hours after a meal.

1. What did you eat?
2. Where and when did you eat?
3. How did you dose insulin at these meals (if applicable)?

What foods do you eat when you feel at your best?

What meals are the easiest for you to manage your diabetes? Why?

What do loved ones currently do to help you make better mealtime choices? What can they start doing? Who can you ask for help?

Look at the answers above. What are your Bright Spots – the things you can try to do more often? How might you encourage them?

Landmine Questions

Think about times when you see out-of-range blood sugars (over 11 mmol/l or less than 4 mmol/l) 2-3 hours after a meal.

1. What did you eat?
2. Where and when did you eat?
3. How did you dose insulin at these meals (if applicable)?

What are your kryptonite foods and snacks – you are powerless over their call, and once you eat a little bit, you go overboard?

What meals are the hardest for you to manage your diabetes? Why?

What foods do you always regret eating? What foods make you feel the worst?

What restaurants or menu items always result in high BGs?

What do loved ones do that encourages unhelpful mealtime choices?

Look at the answers above. What are your Landmines – the things you can try to do less often? How might you avoid them?

.

02

Mindset

Finding Motivation and Crushing
Stress, Burnout, and Guilt

CHAPTER SUMMARY

 Mindset

MY BRIGHT SPOTS | p. 90

- Why does an in-range blood sugar benefit me TODAY: better mood, relationships, energy levels
- BG numbers are neutral information to make a decision; they are not "good" or "bad" grades or "tests"
- Rely on loved ones and friends for support, remember my diabetes affects them too, and communicate about what is helpful
- Gratitude for what I have and how far diabetes has come; I have a duty to take care of myself
- Take 5-10 minutes for deep breaths in the morning (mindfulness)
- Use the "zoom out" visualization to put stress into perspective. Will I remember this moment in a year?
- Change my immediate environment to make better choices easier or unhelpful choices harder
- Set process goals with mini-milestones: focus on consistency and routine, not outcomes
- There are only 24 hours in a day and I can only do my best
- Commit to a goal and hold myself accountable: tell friends, make it public, lock myself in financially

MY LANDMINES | p. 120

- Perfectionist mindset, unrealistic BG expectations, obsessing about things I cannot control
- Unproductive, deflating, blaming questions: Why am I so terrible at this? Why is this not working? Could diabetes be any worse? How could I make the same mistake again?

QUESTIONS TO ASK YOURSELF | p. 129

MY MINDSET BRIGHT SPOTS

 Why does an in-range blood sugar benefit me TODAY: better mood, relationships, energy levels

Why is diabetes worth caring about? Why go through the trouble of eating differently, exercising, taking my medicine, needle pokes, and doctor's visits?

> *"Avoid long-term diabetes complications: blindness, amputation, kidney failure, and heart disease."*

This *is* a critical reason to take care of my diabetes, but it has a huge problem: it is often not a great motivator to work hard at taking care of myself *today*. Complications are a far-in-the-future, vague cloud of doom. It's hard to envision how my small decisions today will lead to really bad outcomes in many years.

In fact, it's far easier to say, "I'll have dessert or skip my medication just this once. What's the harm? I'll get back on the path tomorrow."

The solution to this motivation trap is one of the most important Bright Spots in this book, and it requires a time swap:

Why is managing my BG, eating healthier, or exercising important to me __TODAY__? Why does it matter right now?

When my blood sugar is in range (4-8 mmol/l), I know that:

- I'm a kinder, more patient person with the people around me (especially those I love the most).
- I have more energy to do things that make me happy.
- I smile more and am less stressed.
- I sleep better.
- I can think more clearly, and thus, help more people with diabetes through higher quality work at *diaTribe*.

In other words, keeping my BG in range makes me a better human being today and maximizes my limited time on this planet. That is priceless.

Out-of-range blood sugars, by contrast, make everything in my life harder and less enjoyable – I'm tired, grumpy, lightheaded, a worse sleeper, an impaired thinker, and an all-around worse human being. I deserve better, and so do the people around me.

The word "unmotivated" is thrown around a lot in diabetes, particularly at those who are struggling to manage their BGs. I think this is lame and inaccurate.

Instead, I'd argue many people with diabetes are "wrongly motivated" – a fear-based, far-in-the-future reason to take care of an invisible disease simply isn't compelling. Instead, I wish TODAY reasons to keep BG in-range were more widely used – they are more inspiring, more immediate, and more motivating.

When I was diagnosed 15 years ago, someone should have said, "Hey

Adam, keeping your BG in range will make you a better student, a better athlete, a better brother, and a better human being - today!" Had someone said that, maybe I would have taken my diabetes more seriously.

WHAT HELPS ME

PAIR HOW I FEEL AND ACT WITH WHAT MY BG ACTUALLY IS. HOW DO I FEEL WHEN MY BG IS OUT OF RANGE?

CGM is the most powerful tool for understanding this relationship, but a glucose meter works great too. (For those without access to CGM or more strips, try checking BG more frequently for just one week.) I try to link each BG to how I feel at that point in time. What is my mood, energy, and thinking like at 3 mmol/l versus 6 mmol/l versus 14 mmol/l?

WHEN DIABETES FEELS OVERWHELMING AND EXHAUSTING, ASK: "HOW DO IN-RANGE BLOOD SUGARS BENEFIT ME NOW OR TODAY?" THE IDEAL ANSWERS ARE SPECIFIC, SHORT-TERM, AND INVOLVE PEOPLE I LOVE.

Review these reasons often: a Post-It in my BG meter case, a weekly calendar reminder, the background on a computer screen, a page in a journal, etc. When I just want to blow off diabetes, coming back to my "why" is a great pick-me-up. Frequently rotating the reminder location and method helps keep it fresh and top of mind.

BG numbers are neutral information to make a decision; they are not "good" or "bad" grades or "tests"

When I see numbers like that, it's easy to feel like I'm getting a "bad grade" or "failing" with my diabetes. Of course, this is the default interpretation when it's called a BG "TEST."

I neutralize these negative, blaming, self-critical feelings with a simple Mindset Bright Spot:

BG numbers are NOT good or bad.
They are just information to make a decision.
No judgment, no blame.

Or as my friend and diabetes advocate Jeff Hitchcock recently told me,

"The only 'bad' blood sugar is the one you don't know."

A speedometer in a car indicates if I'm going too fast or too slow, at which point I change how I'm driving (i.e., more gas or more brake). The number on my meter is a speedometer for my diabetes – change my medication, go for a walk, make a different food choice next time, etc. In other words, a 14 mmol/l or a 2.4 mmol/l is a neutral data point to drive an action. Once I get frustrated and attach grades to BG numbers, it's easy to feel like a failure, or worse, to skip the "TEST" altogether.

The Behavioral Diabetes Institute actually recommends putting a sticky note on your meter that says, "It's just a number." I love that!

When I was diagnosed, BG numbers did feel like a grade, which drove me to check less often, and in turn, spend less time in range.

I wish someone had likened diabetes to flying a plane from San Francisco to Sydney: would I trust a pilot using only three GPS readings over the course of a 15-hour flight? Or would I feel safer on a plane flown with GPS information updated every few minutes, plus trend arrows to guide safe flying?

More frequent data and trending information:

1. Confirms the plane is flying smoothly; or
2. Shows the plane is NOT flying smoothly and a course correction is needed.

No pilot in the world views GPS readings as a value judgment: "You are a bad pilot." The plane's current location is *information to drive an action.*

Diabetes is no different! Frequent BG data points are my friend and help me navigate the daily diabetes journey safely:

"I'M IN-RANGE NOW" or "I'M VERY LIKELY TO BE IN RANGE SOON"	"I'M OUT OF RANGE NOW" or "I'M LIKELY TO BE OUT OF RANGE SOON"
→ Do nothing.	→ Change something.

WHAT HELPS ME

TRANSFORM HOW I VIEW BG NUMBERS:

They are <u>neutral</u> data points to take action, not grades on my performance. This concept is so underappreciated in diabetes. Dr. Trang Ly, one of the smartest and most empathetic endocrinologists I know, has another good analogy to describe the unfairness of judging BG numbers:

> *"How would you feel if you were judged on your weight, if you were told it was a 'good' or a 'bad' number, and if you were made to weigh yourself multiple times per day? That's the stigma and guilt people with diabetes have to deal with."*

ADD "IT'S JUST A NUMBER" to my BG meter or CGM, or simply remind myself often.

EXPLAIN THIS CONCEPT TO LOVED ONES, who can help raise my spirits and take the big picture view when I'm sinking into self-blame mode.

Rely on loved ones and friends for support, remember my diabetes affects them too, and honestly communicate about what is helpful

One of my major Mindset Bright Spots comes from loved ones, family, and friends: they lift my motivation when I feel deflated, help me make better food choices and avoid unhelpful options, provide a sounding board to vent frustrations, exercise with me, and even gently nudge me to relax ("Adam, it's just a number; don't be frustrated. I still love you").

WITH MY FIVE YOUNGER SIBLINGS

Unfortunately, these same individuals can also turn into "Diabetes Police" quite easily: "What's your number? Did you go for a walk? How could you mess up again?" I've found diabetes co-exists with relationships when at least four things are in place:

 A strong understanding of how hard it is to live with diabetes. When loved ones are surprised by an out-of-range BG value, I often talk about all the factors (22+!) that affect each blood sugar. Sharing just how much complexity goes into every number brings an appreciation of how much work diabetes requires and how frustrating it can be. (See the Mindset Landmine on perfectionism for more on this.)

2   **Do not use BG numbers to finger point.** The value on the meter is for learning and action, not a performance evaluation.

3   **Open communication:** nothing is worse than when one person is angry or frustrated and doesn't let the other person know.

4   **The person with diabetes should set clear boundaries and acceptable ways of interacting.** For example, "I don't appreciate when you comment on my food choices; please leave those to me" versus "Yes, please help me with my food choices and please stop me from eating junk food." It also helps to clarify when someone has crossed the line: "I know you mean well, but when you comment or judge my numbers, it makes me feel like a failure. Instead, what about helping me with the action step? 'Let's take a walk' or 'Here are some glucose tablets.'"

Those around me cannot read my mind – I must give clear and honest feedback. Where do I need the most help? What is unhelpful?

> *"The single biggest problem in communication is the illusion that it has taken place."*
>
> **GEORGE BERNARD SHAW**

I find support is most helpful around eating and hypoglycemia. Food is such a social activity that the people around me can make a truly meaningful difference. For example, I give my girlfriend full permission to prevent me from eating junk food. It also helps that we don't buy Landmine foods when going to the store, and we cook low-carb dinners together at home. These are meaningful sacrifices she makes to keep me healthy. But support matters in small ways too: whether it's asking if I have glucose tabs before we leave the house, or waking me up to a CGM alarm at night, I know she has my back.

Even still, I constantly have to remind myself that **there is no badge of honor for doing diabetes alone**. As Dr. Brenè Brown says beautifully in *The Gifts of Imperfection*:

> *"Somehow we've come to equate success with not needing anyone. Many of us are willing to extend a helping hand, but we're very reluctant to reach out for help when we need it ourselves. It's as if we've divided the world into 'those who offer help' and 'those who need help.' The truth is that we are both."*[24]

WHAT HELPS ME

BE BRAVE AND HAVE AN HONEST CONVERSATION WITH LOVED ONES, FAMILY AND FRIENDS:

What can they start or stop doing to help me, even in small ways? What does a loved one say that is super motivating and helpful? What is harmful or de-motivating? Where am I struggling the most with my diabetes right now, and how can those around me support me? Do I need help with food choices, an exercise partner, stress reduction, etc.?

ENCOURAGE A LOVED ONE OR FRIEND TO DO A "DAY OF DIABETES" - taking fingersticks and medications, wearing a pump or CGM, doing diabetes math, resisting tempting foods, etc.

A SUPPORT GAMECHANGER

How to Connect with Other People Who Have Diabetes

The diabetes community – online and in person – is a terrific place to find support, learn tips and tricks, and stay up to date on the newest research and products. Many people find peer support an essential part of their diabetes care, no different from the medicine they take.

SOCIAL MEDIA

FIND FACEBOOK GROUPS OR PAGES RELATED TO DIABETES THAT INTEREST YOU:

Groups are often closed and allow for more intimate comments and questions, while pages are usually from organizations and tend to share more news and updates. If you search "diabetes" on Facebook and sort by pages or groups, you can browse and find those relevant to your needs (e.g., by diabetes type, gender, location, etc.). I recommend "Liking" many pages and joining several groups so you can see what sticks; you can always leave one that is not a fit. Our *diaTribe* page is at **facebook.com/ diaTribeNews**

GET ON TWITTER TO FIND PEOPLE WITH DIABETES AND ORGANIZATIONS:

Searching #diabetes, #T1D, and #T2D is one way to find and follow those tweeting about diabetes. The more you use Twitter, the more it will recommend others with diabetes to follow. Many live Twitter chats take place throughout the week too, including #DSMA, #DCDE, #GBDOC, and many others. You can find *diaTribe* on Twitter at **twitter.com/diaTribeNews**

DIABETES ONLINE COMMUNITIES AND WEBSITES

Go to **http://diatribe.org/diabetes-blogs-and-forums** for a list of websites, communities, and online resources. Try out many of these sites; just like apps, some will stick and others won't fit.

IN-PERSON EVENTS

Conferences, local events, and fundraisers are a great way to meet fellow people with diabetes. Organizations like ADA, Children with Diabetes (Friends for Life), JDRF, TCOYD, and many others host terrific in-person events; I always learn something new, and many are free or low cost. I've had the most fun at diabetes charity bike rides – they are a great way to get outside, meet others touched by diabetes, and raise money for a larger cause. These events also make you feel special for having diabetes, a pretty rare and awesome feeling. I'll never forget one of my rides with ADA, where strangers excitedly cheered me on, just because I was wearing the jersey pictured above.

 Gratitude for what I have and how far diabetes has come; I have a duty to take care of myself

"Trade your expectations for appreciation."

TONY ROBBINS

When I'm feeling frustrated and having a tough diabetes day, I try to remember how lucky I am - it always puts my challenges in perspective.

I try to think about places in the world where diabetes is still a death sentence, or when people live for years with diabetes not even knowing they have it, or those who cannot access even the most basic medications to stay alive.

Dr. David Kendall once said in *diaTribe*, "The tools and resources available for you to care for your diabetes in the midst of a busy, productive, and fulfilling life are better today than at any time in the modern history of diabetes care."[25]

Indeed, only a few decades ago, people with diabetes had stone age tools to manage BG: urine monitoring only gave a *range* of BG values that represented glucose hours before; insulins were far less predictable and caused more dangerous lows; syringes needed to be manually sharpened and boiled; and most important, there wasn't even a study to prove that better glucose control reduces the risk of complications.

Before insulin was discovered, diabetes was truly a death sentence: the best treatment at the time, a starvation diet, only delayed the inevitable.[26]

I would happily give diabetes up in a second, but since it's part of my journey, I have a duty - to myself, to loved ones, to society - to do the best I can with the tools and resources at my disposal.

I'm lucky to have access to therapies and care that keep me healthy, which is unfortunately not true for many people around the world.

Tough diabetes day or not, I *must* be grateful for what I have and strive to do my best.

One strategy that has really helped me in recent months is The Five Minute Journal (**intelligentchange.com**), a tip I picked up from author Tim Ferriss.

This little book has made me happier, less stressed, and more reflective and grateful every day - it's easily the best $23 I've spent in a long time. I now start and end the day in a more positive and reflective mindset.

Each page in the journal corresponds to a day, half of which is dedicated to the morning and half to the evening. As the page to the right shows, the questions are easy to answer - the morning questions set the tone for the day, while the nightly questions recap what went well (Bright Spots) and could have been better (Landmines). I usually end up writing at least one actionable health-related thing I want to do or wish I had done that day (e.g.,

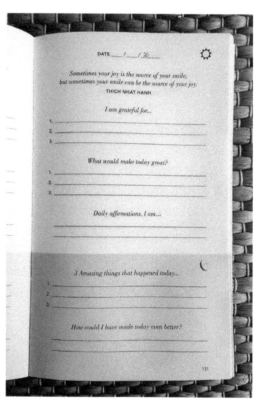

take a bike ride, snack less, etc.). I have tried "gratitude" apps in the past - given the strong link to greater happiness and joy[27] - but none ever stuck. This handwritten journal has me hooked, and I have barely missed an entry in the six months of using it thus far. On tough days, it's also fantastic to thumb back through the journal and realize how many good things I have going in my life. Bright Spots are easier to find when I'm recording and reviewing them!

USE *THE FIVE MINUTE JOURNAL* EVERY DAY.

I keep it next to my bed as a reminder to fill it out first thing when I wake up and the last thing I do before sleep. I really try to vary my daily answers to the "I am grateful for…" question; otherwise, I end up putting the same few generic things every day.

FOCUS ON GRATITUDE WITH A LOVED ONE.

My girlfriend and I started the journal together and hold each other accountable. "How was your day? What was your favorite journal entry?" Plus, with two journals lying around the house, there are more cues to remember to fill it out.

LEARN ABOUT DIABETES AROUND THE WORLD THROUGH the International Diabetes Federation and Life for a Child (**idf.org/lifeforachild**), Team Type 1 (**teamtype1.org**), AYUDA (**ayudainc.net**), and other organizations. The teams behind these organizations do remarkable work, and it always puts my (small) diabetes challenges into perspective.

Take 5-10 minutes for deep breaths in the morning (mindfulness)

"The present moment is so underrated."

ANDY PUDDICOMBE, FOUNDER OF HEADSPACE

Taking just 5-10 minutes in the morning to breathe deeply ("mindfulness" or "meditation") is a key Mindset Bright Spot for easing into my day, improving my patience, and reducing my stress.

I think of mindfulness as a useful diabetes tool, since stress can cause high BGs, and high BGs can cause stress. Morning breathing can help in both cases.

The return-on-investment with mindfulness is amazing - even five minutes at 7:30 am can make an immediate difference in the morning (when I open up my email inbox) and a lasting difference at 4:30 pm (when a last-minute, unexpected project hits at work).

Mindfulness felt intimidating, uncomfortable, weird, and very difficult at first – I'm still not good at it, but the resources listed below have helped me sprinkle a few deep breaths into the craziness of daily life. Guided audio tracks and mindfulness apps have been personal Bright Spots - it's like having a personal teacher built into my phone.

But of all the habits I've tried to integrate into my life, this has been one of the most difficult. I know the benefits, but often feel too tired or too busy in the morning to take time to breathe. Sometimes I just forget.

It's still a constant work in progress, but here's what I've picked up along the way:

1 **Learn the ropes from an app, device, or book (see page 106) and be patient** - like learning an instrument or playing a new sport, mindfulness takes time and is initially frustrating and awkward.

2 **Start incredibly small: one minute per day for a week. Even I can spare one minute!** I've heard some recommend playing a favorite song and simply focusing on breathing in and out until the song ends.

③ Pair mindfulness with something I *already* do every day, ideally at the same time - for example, waiting for water to boil to make morning tea, commuting to work, or walking my dog. This is a great way to start a new behavior, since the existing behavior serves as the "trigger" or "anchor." Usually I take deep breaths while my hot water for tea boils, since it's something I do every single morning.

④ Find a consistent time and location. I prefer mindfulness in the morning because it's slightly easier to remember, it's quieter, and I can do it before checking email and becoming reactive. It's like filling up my gas tank before I start the day.

⑤ Identify the benefits of mindfulness and remember them when I'm about to skip it for the day. When I take time to breathe in the morning, I'm a:

- Better person with loved ones, coworkers, and strangers;
- Less stressed and anxious at work;
- Less disrupted by the small diabetes and life hiccups that happen every day;
- More joyful, grateful, and happy person.

⑥ Use a habit tracking app (e.g., Coach.me, Way of Life, Productive, Momentum, Streaks) or a paper calendar to "check in" once I've completed my deep breathing session. This defines success as consistency, a big boost for starting new behaviors. I find check-in apps are hard to sustain long-term, but they are helpful for getting off the ground. Putting X's on an old-fashioned paper calendar works well too.

Related to morning breathing, I also try to maximize activities that keep me in the moment ("flow") instead of worrying about the past or future. For me, this includes conversations with loved ones and friends, exercise and time outside, reading, writing, listening to music and podcasts, and games. The more present-oriented activities I build into my day, the less time I have to stress and worry about all my to-dos. During these activities, I try to put my phone on do-not-disturb (or turn my laptop's wifi off using the Freedom app) to avoid interruptions.

WHAT HELPS ME

APPS:

- **BUDDHIFY (www.buddhify.com; Apple and Android)** | Buddhify includes over 80 guided soundtracks chosen based on the environment I'm in: "At work," "Before bed," "Can't sleep" "Walking," etc. I love the waking up ("Good") and going to sleep ("Thanks") tracks.
- **CALM (www.calm.com; Apple, Android, and web)** | The variety of nature sounds is fantastic.
- **HEADSPACE (www.headspace.com; Apple and Android)** | Headspace includes a free Take 10 program (10 minutes for 10 days), with a lot of explanation and great animations. The app has more than 3 million users in over 150 countries.

DEVICES:

- **APPLE WATCH AND FITBIT RECENTLY ADDED BREATHE FEATURES**, showing an onscreen animation to guide mindful breathing. This feature makes breathing more accessible (right on the wrist) and engaging, and it reduces the bar for completing it (just a minute or two).

BOOKS:

- *MINDFULNESS IN PLAIN ENGLISH* | by Bhante Henepola Gunaratana – A highly informative how-to book on the basics of mindfulness, with over a quarter of a million copies sold.
- *WAY OF THE PEACEFUL WARRIOR* | by Dan Millman – One of my favorite books and something I try to re-read once

per year. It's a story rather than a how-to-guide, but it always reminds me how to live a more mindful and present-oriented life.

- **ANYTHING WRITTEN BY** Thich Nhat Hanh, Tara Brach, or Jon Kabat-Zinn.

 Use the "zoom out" visualization to put stress into perspective. Will I remember this moment in a year?

"Worry is like a rocking chair, it will give you something to do, but it won't get you anywhere."

VANCE HAVNER

It's so easy to get stressed, worried, or frustrated at the smallest things, particularly diabetes hassles: a high BG when "I did everything right" or when I did the same thing yesterday and ended up low. That stress can then cause *further* high BGs, perpetuating the cycle.

One Mindset Bright Spot I love is called the "zoom out" visualization, as described in *The Charisma Myth* by Olivia Fox-Cabane.[28]

In my head, I zoom out to see planet Earth hanging in space. Then I zoom in to see my continent, my country, my city, my street, my house, and then the room I'm in. I imagine myself sitting in that room, with little electrical pulses whizzing across my brain. I'm one person having one stressful experience in this moment.

This visualization usually puts my anxiety and worries in the right perspective - small! - particularly when I think about all the people going through much tougher times.

99.9% of my stress is not a big deal in the grand scheme of my life. "Will I remember this moment in a year? Will this affect anything truly important?" Usually, the answer is a firm "No!"

I find it a relief to take this 10,000-foot view, to realize that the minor daily hiccups – a high morning BG, a low during exercise, a frustrating experience with my insurance company or doctor – are not worth getting upset over.

"Subconsciously, we should be constantly asking ourselves this question: Do I need to freak out about this?"

RYAN HOLIDAY *in* **THE OBSTACLE IS THE WAY**

WHAT HELPS ME

FIND WAYS TO "ZOOM OUT," WHICH CAN TAKE MANY FORMS:

The visualization noted on the previous page, glancing up at the stars or moon or clouds, looking out at the ocean, hiking in forests or mountains, etc. Remembering the incredible passage of time and my place in the huge universe helps put things in perspective – my "problems" are usually not a big deal.

Change my immediate environment to make better choices easier or unhelpful choices harder

"Many people have discovered that, when it comes to changing their own behavior, environmental tweaks beat self-control every time."

CHIP AND DAN HEATH *in* **SWITCH**

Assuming I have infallible willpower and infinite motivation is never a good strategy – I prove myself wrong time and time again.

One of my favorite Mindset Bright Spots takes advantage of my immediate surroundings, which have a big, but hidden, impact on my diabetes choices. My goal is always to structure my environment so that my Bright Spots happen more often and more automatically – no willpower needed (ideally).

How can I set up my environment to make the right choices easier or make the wrong choices harder? Here are some examples I've used successfully:

BRIGHT SPOT CHOICE
EASIER:

LANDMINE CHOICE
HARDER:

- Placing my glucose meter next to my bed so I always check when I wake up and before sleep.
- Carrying around a water bottle so I remember to drink more water.
- Setting up a small home gym so I can exercise even when I don't have time to go to the gym.
- Use smaller dinner plates so I eat less food (8 inches across).
- Use an enormous salad bowl (the size of my head) so I automatically eat more veggies.

- No junk foods in the house, or at minimum, hidden from sight. If crackers, chips, candy, and sugar are really hard to access, they will be harder to eat.
- Unplugging and storing our small projector and video games in a crate, so when I want to play or watch, I have to take 7 minutes to set everything up.
- Fill up on vegetables, water, tea, or broth at dinner so I'm less likely to overeat Landmine foods.
- In restaurants, ask the waiter not to serve me bread, rice, or pasta, substituting vegetables instead.

I love that these environment changes are small but can meaningfully impact my behavior and "save me from myself."

We all use environment tweaks already for every day, mundane things: storing car keys or a wallet in the same place (easier to find, less likely to lose), placing an umbrella by the front door when rain is expected tomorrow, and even automatic bill payment.

For me, the fun part of this Bright Spot has been trying many different experiments. Where should things be placed in the house as reminders? Can I try different daily schedules and see what impact it has on my behavior?

What is the "automatic bill pay" environment tweak that will help me exercise more often?

It might be setting up a home gym, parking farther from the office, taking the stairs whenever possible, or putting my bike next to the front door – the possibilities are endless, and when I pick the right option(s), my BGs and mental outlook often improve too.

There is no one-size-fits-all environment change, but there is immense variety here, it doesn't take much to change my behavior, and many approaches don't cost anything.

WHAT HELPS ME

ANALYZE MY ENVIRONMENT AND BEHAVIOR LIKE A DETECTIVE:

When I make the right choices, what in my surroundings enabled that? When I make the wrong choices, what could I have done differently to setup my immediate environment?

RUN PERSONAL EXPERIMENTS WITH DIFFERENT ROUTINES, OBJECT PLACEMENT, BEHAVIORAL CUES, ETC.

Keep asking, "Did this change make the right choice easier or the wrong choices harder?"

Set process goals with mini-milestones: focus on consistency and routine, not outcomes

> 01 *"Get an A1c less than 7% by April 1."*

> 02 *"Cycle 1,000 miles this year."*

> 03 *"Check blood glucose before and 2–3 hours after meals and take action on each number."*

> 04 *"Ride my bike on Tuesdays, Thursdays, and Saturdays."*

These are all valuable goals, but they are different. The first two are what I call "outcomes" goals, while the third and fourth are "process" goals.

A lot of goal setting focuses on outcomes: what is my end destination? This can provide useful motivation, but I find it often leaves the journey too unclear. These "outcome" goals can also make me feel like a failure if I fall short.

One of my motivation Bright Spots relies on setting process goals: the interim step of doing something rather than the need to hit an outcome. It's the journey mindset, not the destination vision. For example, checking blood sugar before and after every meal or riding my bike three times every week. Emphasizing the process can ensure the larger goal is served (e.g., an A1c less than 7%, cycling 1,000 miles this year), but with less pressure to hit an outcome.

I also like that process goals clarify the journey in more actionable ways - "check blood glucose before and after meals" is more useful than "get an A1c less than 7%."

The key to this Bright Spot, of course, is choosing the right process goal. What interim step(s) will ensure my larger goal is served? Which single step, if completed consistently, would make the biggest difference to my larger goal?

Sometimes, getting started at all is the hardest part. I often ask:

"What is the absolute smallest step I can take right now to move forward?"

Even though it feels unambitious, I have to force myself to think tiny and specific – what can be done in the next five minutes? In the next one hour on a commute? In an afternoon? This week? Focusing on the immediate next step – even when it is small – is often enough to boost my motivation to tackle a big goal, and from there, it can snowball!

A journey of a thousand miles begins with a single step. Just. One. Step. Examples:

- Eat one extra vegetable at my upcoming meal.
- Go for a five-minute walk around the block right now.
- Put my exercise clothes on.
- Check my blood sugar one extra time today.
- Breathe for one minute this morning.
- Floss one tooth today (a funny recommendation from Stanford's Dr. BJ Fogg).[29]

Then, the key is replicating that small step over and over again to build momentum and actually feel progress.

I set a goal a couple years ago to bike 3,000 miles for the year, a very ambitious 50% increase over the prior year. The only way I achieved the big goal was breaking it down into weekly sub-goals (60 miles per week), and from there, a process goal: two short bike rides during the week and a long ride on the weekend. That narrowing, or reframe, made the huge goal so much more achievable.

Another example is the book you are reading. Even though I write every day for a living, the thought of writing this book was truly daunting. I didn't get going until I broke it down into smaller steps that felt doable.

Diabetes is no different – just one more Bright Spot (checking BG after meals) or one fewer Landmine (hypoglycemia binge) every day can make a big difference on the journey to more in-range BGs and higher quality of life.

WHAT HELPS ME

THE TINY STEP I *ACTUALLY* TAKE ALWAYS BEATS THE HUGE STEP I *DREAM* ABOUT TAKING BUT NEVER DO. ASK, "WHAT IS THE SMALLEST STEP I CAN TAKE RIGHT NOW TO WORK TOWARD THE LARGER VISION?"

If I can't come up with anything, it helps to reach out to someone else for perspective and ideas.

BREAK A BIG OUTCOME GOAL INTO A PROCESS: "TWO SHORT WEEKDAY BIKE RIDES AND ONE LONG WEEKEND RIDE" INSTEAD OF "RIDE 3,000 MILES THIS YEAR."

These process milestones should be small, specific, and near-term. Experimenting with different process goals (time frames, types of goals) can help arrive at the right solution.

JOIN DR. BJ FOGG'S "TINY HABITS" PROGRAM (tinyhabits.com /join)

It's free and done over email. The five-day behavior change program takes less than 30 minutes total and helps users "tap the power of environment and baby steps." I loved it! Make sure to read the fascinating intro document.

IDENTIFY MY BIGGEST BARRIER(S). HAVE A PARTNER OR FRIEND ASK THE FOLLOWING QUESTIONS, AND FILL IN THE BLANKS WITH MY OWN RESPONSES.

The answer to the last question is the key barrier that needs to be addressed. I picked this up from Chip and Dan Heath's terrific behavior change book, *Switch*.

PARTNER

On a scale of 1 to 10, how ready are you to _____.
(insert desired goal).

E.g. "On a scale of 1 to 10, how ready are you to start exercising 30 minutes each day?"

ME

I'm a ___ out of 10. (Insert a # from 1–10, with 10 being 'very ready' and 1 'not at all ready').

E.g. "I'm a <u>6</u> out of <u>10</u>."

PARTNER

What would need to happen for you to go from a ____ (current number) to _____ (higher number)?

E.g. "What would need to happen for you to go from a <u>6</u> to a <u>7</u>?"

ME

I would need to _____.

E.g. "I would need to find someone to walk with me after work."

There are only 24 hours in a day and I can only do my best

When I'm feeling the daunting weight of professional, personal, and diabetes stress on my shoulders, two related Bright Spot thoughts often rescue me:

1. There are only 24 hours in a day: I can't do everything perfectly.
2. I can only do my best.

These combined insights help calm some of the biggest drivers of diabetes and life anxiety: What if I can't do it all? What if I fall short? What if I'm not good enough?

Stress often feels like a time problem: how am I going to spend time with my loved ones and friends, do a great job on work I care about, cook meals at home, exercise, sleep enough, take care of my diabetes, AND have fun?

As my sister likes to say, "You can't level up in every area of your life."

All of us want to be like that perfect video game character who has mastered every skill. But it's impossible.

For a perfectionist achiever like me, this is actually a liberating thought. I have to make choices.

Instead of trying to become a Jedi Master in every part of my life, what should I focus on now? What systems can I set up to let other areas run on auto-pilot? **What activities have ripple effects that will make the rest of my day easier?**

For example, getting ten minutes of exercise, at least seven hours of sleep, and breathing for 5-10 minutes in the morning help me accomplish all other tasks. The ripple effect alone makes them worth doing every day.

WHAT HELPS ME

WHEN THE TO-DO LIST IS OVERWHELMING AND A WAVE OF STRESS HITS, RESPOND WITH, "[Deep breath] There are only 24 hours today. I can only do my best. [Deep breath]"

WHAT ACTIVITIES GIVE THE BIGGEST QUALITY-OF-LIFE PAYOFF RELATIVE TO THE TIME INVESTMENT?

What can I put on auto-pilot to free up my time for more life-enhancing activities? (e.g., online subscriptions for groceries, automatic diabetes supply shipments, automatic bill pay, etc.)

WHAT AREA(S) OF MY LIFE ARE BRINGING ME DOWN THE MOST RIGHT NOW? WHAT IS ONE EXPERIMENT I CAN TRY THIS WEEK?

Who has gone through this before that might help me?

Commit to a goal and hold myself accountable: tell friends, make it public, lock myself in financially

It's amazing how pledging myself to do something – be it a charity cycling event, checking my blood glucose after every meal, or even walking 20 minutes before breakfast every day – can boost my motivation.

But three days in, things often fall short. "Oh right. That goal... But I'm busy today. Maybe tomorrow?"

Unfortunately, a list of "tomorrows" can easily pile up into a list of "never-done-at-alls."

Public commitment is one Bright Spot I've used to overcome this trap. How can I make my goal public, adding social, financial, or personal pressure to complete it? Can I lock myself in so that achieving the goal is more likely? For example:

- Tell my friends and family about a goal, ask them to hold me accountable (or even better, to join me!), and figure out a positive reward for completing it.
- Post my goal on social media, write it on a blog, or find other ways to make it public.
- Use goal-tracking websites like **www.stickk.com** to make a commitment and set "stakes" - for example, sending my money to an "anti-charity" (an organization I don't support) if I don't achieve my goal.

I actually used **Stickk.com** to complete the first draft of this book, and believe me, the stakes of donating to a political "anti-charity" that I did not support were unbelievably effective. My girlfriend served as my "referee" - meaning I couldn't cheat it - and I told coworkers and friends about my goal to further lock myself in socially.

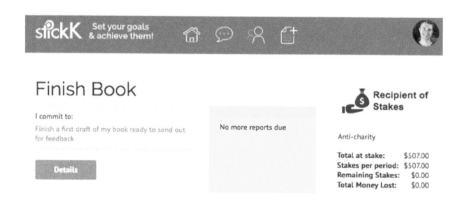

This idea of public commitment is rooted in psychology, which has proven that we are all naturally swayed by the "consistency principle." As Dr. Robert Cialdini's classic book *Influence* notes, "Once we have made a choice or taken a stand, we will encounter personal and interpersonal pressures to behave consistently with that commitment."

WHAT HELPS ME

CHOOSE SOMETHING I REALLY CARE ABOUT ACHIEVING.

If my heart is not in it, the most public commitment won't matter. (In fact, it can backfire.)

LOCK MYSELF IN FINANCIALLY, SOCIALLY, OR PERSONALLY. HOW CAN I PUT MYSELF ON THE LINE?

For instance, if my goal is to walk every day, what better way than to find a partner, to raise money for diabetes research, or to adopt a dog? Commitment falls along a spectrum from minimal to epic; how much does this goal mean to me, and how can I escalate the commitment so I have no choice but to do it?

MY MINDSET LANDMINES

 Perfectionist mindset, unrealistic BG expectations, obsessing about things I cannot control

Self-criticism, guilt, and frustration assault me all the time, and they stem from the same Mindset Landmine: perfectionism.

Perfectionism can exist in a predictable world where 1+1 always equals 2. With diabetes, 1+1 sometimes equals 2, but often it equals 4,000 or -10.

My perfectionist streak sets unrealistic expectations for living with diabetes. I'm trying to replicate what the human body without diabetes does so elegantly – perfect glucose sensing in seconds, the perfect amount of insulin delivery in seconds in the perfect location (the liver, not under the skin), and perfectly functioning hormones like glucagon (to prevent hypoglycemia) and amylin (to prevent a spike in blood sugar after meals).

When I'm striving for perfection, or frustrated when I'm not achieving it, I try to remember how much of diabetes is out of my control, even when I'm doing my best: there are more than 22 factors that affect blood glucose (see the following pages or **diaTribe.org/factors**). When I realized this, I breathed a sigh of relief. I do NOT have *complete* control over every BG.

Sometimes the food has more carbs than I guessed, or the vial of insulin or infusion set is not working well, or I'm sick, or my meter isn't reading accurately, or at least 15 other things. Some of these individual variables are manageable, but all of these factors interact in infinitely complicated ways: what happens to my BG after five hours of sleep, a low-carb breakfast, lots of exercise, high stress, and the second day of my infusion set? I cannot possibly predict that!

Encouraging my Diabetes Bright Spots and avoiding my Landmines helps enormously, but it still won't eliminate ALL out-of-range BGs. **And that is okay.**

For insulin users, the current tools to manage diabetes make perfection nearly impossible. As just one example, imagine a car with a 60-90-minute lag between steering the wheel and the car meaningfully changing direction, and a full three hours or more before the car stops turning. It would be ridiculously difficult to drive safely. But that is the *same* delay we have with current injected rapid-acting insulins: a 60-90 minute delay before they peak, and a duration of action that lasts three hours or more. Keeping the car on the road - my BG in-range - is tough with that kind of steering wheel!

There are definite benefits to striving for perfection: giving 100% effort, constantly trying to improve, and sticking to my goals. But expecting diabetes perfection is simply unrealistic, or as I like to say...

"Perfectionism is a good servant but a bad master."

KEEP A HEALTHY PERSPECTIVE. PERFECT, NON-DIABETES BLOOD SUGARS ARE CHALLENGING TO ACHIEVE, GIVEN: (i) the number of factors that affect blood sugar; (ii) the current tools we have to manage diabetes; and (iii) the need not to spend every minute of every day on diabetes.

TAKE ACTION ON OUT-OF-RANGE BLOOD SUGARS, TRY TO FIGURE OUT WHAT CAUSED THEM (IF POSSIBLE), BUT DO NOT BEAT MYSELF UP FOR FALLING SHORT OF PERFECTION.

I can only do my best, and even then, things will never be perfect.

FOCUS ON THE BIGGEST SOURCES OF VARIABILITY IN DIABETES: food choices and carb counting, medication (especially insulin) doses, and obtaining accurate BG readings (wash hands!).

REMEMBER FRUSTRATION AND SELF-CRITICISM USUALLY MAKE ME FEEL CRAPPY, BUT DON'T TYPICALLY MAKE THINGS BETTER.

As my friend with diabetes Scott Johnson told me:

> *"Learn to appreciate the strength you have – if you've survived even a single day with diabetes, you're stronger than you realize. Think about how a non-diabetic endocrine system works, then compare that to everything you do in order to navigate a day with diabetes. It's amazing, isn't it? We do an incredible job, yet we don't appreciate it often enough."*

HOW MANY FACTORS
Actually AFFECT
BLOOD GLUCOSE

Based on personal experience, conversations with experts, and scientific research, here's a partial list of some of the factors that can affect BG. They are separated into five areas – Food, Medication, Activity, Biological, and Environmental factors. I've provided arrows to show the general effect these factors have on my blood glucose (a sideways arrow indicates a neutral effect), but not every individual will respond in the same way (and even within the same person, you may be different from day-to-day or over time). Certain factors may also apply more to type 1 versus type 2 diabetes (or the other way around).

Factors with up and down arrows are of course the most challenging - I find they sometimes increase my BG and sometimes decrease it. The best way to see how a factor affects you is through personal experience – check your blood glucose more often or wear CGM and look for patterns. Read explanations behind each factor at **diaTribe.org/factors**.

FOOD		BIOLOGICAL	
↑ ↑	1. Carbohydrates	↑	11. Dawn phenomenon
↑	2. Fat	↑	12. Infusion set issues
→ ↑	3. Protein	↑	13. Scar tissue and lipodystrophy
→ ↑	4. Caffeine		
↓ ↑	5. Alcohol	↑	14. Insufficient sleep
		↑	15. Stress and illness
MEDICATION		↑	16. Allergies
→ ↓	6. Medication dose	↑	17. A higher glucose level
↓ ↑	7. Medication timing	↓ ↑	18. Periods (menstruation)
↓ ↑	8. Medication interactions	↑	19. Smoking
ACTIVITY		**ENVIRONMENTAL**	
→ ↓	9. Light exercise	↑	20. Expired insulin
↓ ↑	10. High intensity and moderate exercise	↑	21. Inaccurate BG reading
		?	22. Altitude

In addition to the list above, *diaTribe* readers have emailed me with other factors that seem to affect their BGs: outside temperature, hydration, sunburn, allergic reactions, steroid administration, niacin, and celiac disease. There is also a lot of ongoing research on the impact of gut bacteria ("microbiome") on BGs and insulin sensitivity.

Unproductive, deflating, blaming questions: Why am I so terrible at this? Why is this not working? Could diabetes be any worse? How could I make the same mistake again?

"Quality questions create a quality life."

TONY ROBBINS

Two reactions are always possible:
1. "Seriously? What did I screw up? Why is nothing going right? UGH!"
2. "Got it. What can I do right now to bring this BG into my target range? What can I change next time so that my BG will stay in my target range?"

The first reaction is a Landmine for motivation: self-blaming, negative, frustrated, and unproductive. The second reaction is a Bright Spot: actionable, non-judgmental, learning-oriented, and productive. The only difference is the mindset and point-of-view I bring to the same situation.

This concept extends into so many areas of diabetes, and I find the Landmine questions are particularly toxic for motivation and diabetes happiness.

 EXAMPLES OF
Landmine Questions:

· Why did this happen to me?
· Why is diabetes so unfair?

- How is this blood sugar possible? I've done everything right today!
- Why is this not working?
- How could I be so lame and forget to do that again?
- What things *can't* I do now that I have diabetes?
- Why is this so difficult?
- Why did I do this to myself?
- Why did I eat that?
- What will my _____ say about this? (doctor, mom, husband, etc.)
- Why can't I do anything right?
- Why do I feel so bad?
- What if something goes wrong?
- Why can't I control this?

Focusing on why diabetes is "unfair" or "limiting" is dangerous and unproductive for me – it makes me feel awful, ruins my mood, and offers little hope that tomorrow will be better (after all, I will have diabetes tomorrow...). Most of all, it leaves me in a hole without a rope.

MY GOAL IS ALWAYS TO ASK
Bright Spot Questions:

- What can I learn from this?
- What is one thing going well in my diabetes, even if it's small (checking BG before breakfast)? How can I build on that?
- Is there anything I can do differently tomorrow to keep my BG in range? What are some different choices or experiments I can try this week?
- What am I grateful for?
- What role models can help inspire and guide me to better manage my diabetes?
- How can I enlist friends and loved ones to help me? Who can help me in the online community?

- What can I still do even though I have diabetes?
- What books, websites, and resources can help me improve?
- How can I use my experience to help others?
- How can I run my first 5K? Cycle 25 miles? Learn how to play tennis for the first time?

These Bright Spot questions *motivate action* and propel me forward - what should I do next?

I tend to be an optimist, but when I started listening to the sound of my own diabetes-related questions, I realized how unproductive many of them were – there's a lot of blame and negative self-criticism. Using more motivating questions has made me think and focus on solutions to problems rather than the problems themselves. It's a small but very meaningful difference.

WHAT HELPS ME

PAY ATTENTION TO THE DIABETES-RELATED QUESTIONS I ROUTINELY ASK MYSELF, ESPECIALLY WHEN THINGS AREN'T GOING WELL. AM I ASKING BRIGHT SPOT OR LANDMINE QUESTIONS?

Can I change the wording of my Landmine questions to make them more solutions-oriented and motivating? When I cannot reword them, I try to replace them entirely with some of the Bright Spot questions shown above.

ENLIST LOVED ONES AND FRIENDS TO HELP ME.

When I overreact to an out-of-range blood sugar on my meter, my girlfriend will often bring me back to reality: "It's not worth getting upset over. It is just a number. You're doing your best." Those words are sometimes all I need. Family and friends can help monitor my language and point out when I'm using de-motivating questions and patterns of speech.

IT TAKES TIME, REPETITION, AND VIGILANCE TO MAKE THIS THINKING EFFORTLESS AND AUTOMATIC.

I can't change my whole psychology immediately, and am certainly still working at this every single day.

QUESTIONS TO ASK YOURSELF

 ## Bright Spot Questions

Why is managing blood sugar, eating healthier, or exercising important to you TODAY? How do you feel when your BG is in range (4-8 mmol/l)? How do you act toward those around you?

On days when you are highly motivated to take care of your diabetes, eat well, or exercise, what big or small things do you do? What makes those days different?

The next time you are frustrated with diabetes, what are two productive, uplifting questions you might ask yourself?

What helps you reduce your stress levels? What activities always calm you down?

Look at the answers above. What are your Bright Spots - the things you can try to do more often? How might you encourage them?

Landmine Questions

What unproductive, deflating, blaming questions do you frequently ask, particularly when you are frustrated with diabetes?

Think about days when you are fed up and tired of diabetes. What factors contribute, and which of those factors could be changed?

What in your environment hurts your diabetes motivation? What destroys your ability to make positive choices (food, mindset, exercise, sleep)?

Think about your highest stress days in the past week. What drove those feelings? Which of these factors are changeable?

Look at the answers above. What are your Landmines – the things you can try to do less often? How might you avoid them?

03

Exercise

Avoiding Lows and Highs, Enjoying
Activity, and Overcoming Barriers

CHAPTER SUMMARY

 Exercise

MY BRIGHT SPOTS | p. 136

- Walk, especially after meals and to correct a high BG
- What is my BG now? How much do I expect it to change by the time I finish activity? Should I eat or take insulin?
- Choose activities I find fun and actually want to do. Am I looking forward to exercise tomorrow?
- Find the right before-exercise glucose target, and learn how many carbs are needed to raise BG to that target
- Eliminate the barriers to exercise with home workouts and exercise apps
- Store treatments for low BGs everywhere in my life (glucose tabs), and always carry them during exercise
- Reduce bolus insulin based on activity type (e.g., -75% for endurance exercise, -30% before walking)
- Track activity with a device or an app to add motivation and friendly competition
- Listen to podcasts, audiobooks, or watch something entertaining during exercise
- Schedule activity: "I lift weights on Monday, Wednesday, and Friday mornings. I ride my bike on Tuesday, Thursday, and Sunday afternoons."
- Accountability to an exercise partner, class, or club
- Adopt a dog: I MUST move!

MY LANDMINES | p. 166

- "All or nothing" mentality: "Well, I don't have an hour, so I can't exercise"
- Eating too close to starting exercise: low BG during activity, high BG after activity
- Overeating after exercise
- Poor recovery: failing to stretch, not enough water, not enough sleep
- Focusing on how painful exercise feels while doing it

QUESTIONS TO ASK YOURSELF | p. 176

DEEP DIVE: HOW I DEAL WITH | p. 179
EXERCISE AND APPLYING THE
BG QUESTIONS

MY EXERCISE BRIGHT SPOTS

 Walk, especially after meals and to correct a high BG

Walking is one of my favorite Exercise Bright Spots - it predictably drops blood sugar (especially after meals), helps correct high BGs more quickly than with insulin alone, lifts my spirits, is easy to do, gets me outside, and the time can be combined with other enjoyable activities (calling family, listening to podcasts, deep breathing). Plus, walking is free and can be done anywhere at nearly any time of day.

Without a doubt, walking is one of the most important therapies I use every day to benefit my diabetes, but it's also one of the most underrated.

I was shocked when I began measuring the BG impact of walking - it's surprisingly effective! When I'm strolling on flat ground at a normal pace, my blood sugar typically drops by about 1 mmol/l in 15 minutes, meaning a 30-minute walk can take me from 9 to 7 mmol/l. If I'm walking uphill or have taken some bolus insulin in the past two hours, I see an even bigger impact, often reducing my blood sugar by 2 mmol/l or more in 15 minutes (from 9 to 5 mmol/l in 30 minutes).

Data from over 60,000 walking sessions in Diabetes Hands Foundation's Big Blue Test program (2010-2016) confirm my findings.

Following 14 minutes of moderate walking, the average participant saw their blood glucose drop by an impressive 1.7 mmol/l.[30]

Typical BG responses to walking after post-meal high BGs:

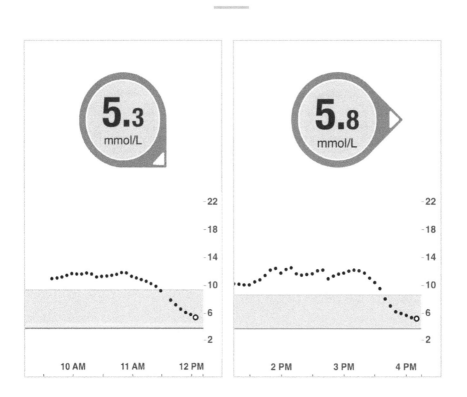

Walking can also reduce the amount of food and correction insulin I need, and in some cases, replace those entirely. A typical insulin dose takes about 60-90 minutes to peak and 3-4 hours to completely finish working. That's *slow!* With a blood sugar of 9.7 mmol/l, I could take three units of insulin and wait 90 minutes for my BG to really start dropping, or I could take a brisk walk for 30 minutes. Even if the walk doesn't bring me all the way back to target, it will usually take me to a lower and safer base from which to correct (e.g., 8.2 mmol/l).

Post-meal walks are particularly effective: I often need about half as much insulin as normal, and in some cases no insulin at all. (The caveat is that I do tend to eat low-carb meals, where my normal bolus is only 1 or 2 units.) When my BG is trending high after a meal, a walk can help course-correct me back into range without adding more insulin.

Last but not least, walking also improves my mood and cuts my stress, which is exactly what I need with a high BG.

WHAT HELPS ME

SNEAK WALKING INTO DAILY ROUTINE:

- **WORK** | Commute, breaks, walking meetings with colleagues, conference calls
- **HOME** | Before breakfast, after dinner, while watching a show or during commercials (pace the living room)
- **SOCIAL** | Weekly catch-up with a friend, phone calls to family
- **ERRANDS** | Park farther away in a parking lot, take the stairs, do extra laps of the grocery store

TRACK DAILY STEPS WITH A DEVICE OR APP.

I used Fitbit for years and more recently have been trying the Apple Watch – both devices are great and there are countless other options too, including many apps that track steps with a phone alone (no separate device needed). The sense of progress and achievement is addicting, and the feedback right on my wrist is especially motivating. (See the Bright Spot later in this chapter.)

ASK FOR A TREADMILL DESK AT WORK (SERIOUSLY) - THERE IS NO EASIER WAY TO BUILD STEPS INTO BUSY WORKDAYS IN FRONT OF A COMPUTER.

We are so lucky to have a treadmill desk in our diaTribe office and it makes getting 10,000 steps per day much easier. It's also my go-to location when I have a high BG during the day, and I often think better and work faster while walking. More employers are investing in wellness and offering perks like treadmill desks, so this may be an option depending on where you work. A home version can be built with a standard treadmill (used is less expensive) and a bit of home assembly. Searching "DIY Treadmill Desk" online brings up lots of examples like **www.thinkspace.com/super -cheap-diy-treadmill-desk.**

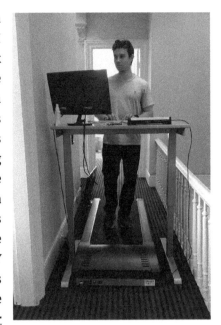

GET A BIKING DESK.

I tried one of these recently at a diabetes company and found it just as useful as a treadmill desk, but way less expensive and less bulky. Fit Desk makes a good option for $299 (**www.thefitdesk. com/bike-desk**). If I had space for a home office in my apartment, this would absolutely be my first purchase.

IF WALKING DOESN'T FEEL LIKE "EXERCISE," TRY IT WITH A WEIGHTED VEST.

I have a 20-lb. option that I often use in the mornings, and it works great for raising my heart rate while I stroll with my dog.

What is my BG now? How much do I expect it to change by the time I finish activity? Should I eat or take insulin?

Understanding and preparing for BG changes during activity is a critical Bright Spot for avoiding lows, highs, and a lot of diabetes frustration. The following three questions take a little planning upfront, but when I go through this thought process, I'm far more likely to stay in range during exercise. The parallels to driving a car - starting destination, ending destination, and road conditions - help me remember the sequence.

1 **What is my BG right now? (What is my starting destination?)** At least 30 minutes before exercise, I take a fingerstick or check my CGM value and trend arrow. This is no different from inputting my starting destination in Google Maps; I have to know my current location to know the driving route.

2 **How much do I expect my BG to change by the time I finish activity? (What is my end destination?)** By checking BGs before and after exercise, I have developed some rough personal guidelines for different activities.

ACTIVITY	TIME	APPROXIMATE BG CHANGE
Walking	30 mins	-2 mmol/l
Biking/Running	30 mins	-3.5 mmol/l
Strength Training	30 mins	No change or slight increase (0 to +2 mmol/l)

(Your guidelines will likely be different, and the "What Helps Me" section below shares tips for developing your own.)

I apply these estimates to my starting BG to get a sense of my expected end destination based on *activity alone.*

For example, with a starting BG of 8 mmol/l, I know a 30-minute walk might take me to about 6 mmol/l, while a 30-minute bike ride might bring me from 8 mmol/l to about 4.5 mmol/l. Of course, some days I see bigger or smaller changes than expected, but on average, these guidelines are a Bright Spot for planning safe exercise.

The end destination often needs to change based on any recent food and bolus insulin: carbs within the last hour may increase my ending BG, while bolus insulin within the last two hours is very likely to drive BG lower. That means instead of going from 8 to 6 mmol/l with a 30-minute walk, I might actually end at 7.5 mmol/l with recent carbs or at 4 mmol/l with recent insulin.

Once I have a rough sense of my expected end destination – including planned activity and any recent food or bolus insulin – I can move on to the last step.

③ Do I need to eat or take some bolus insulin now to: (i) stay in my goal zone of 5.5-10 mmol/l during exercise; and (ii) finish as close to 5.5 mmol/l as possible? (What are the road conditions today?) This is my Bright Spot action for avoiding lows and highs: tweaking my food or bolus insulin (driving) before exercise according to the specific circumstances (road conditions) I'm facing on that day.

For example, from a starting BG of 5.5 mmol/l, a 30-minute bike ride would take me to around 2 mmol/l, a dangerous ending BG. To add some buffer, I'd eat about 15-20 grams of carbs – enough to bring me from my 5.5 mmol/l start up to around 9 mmol/l, right before 30 minutes of riding drops me back down close to my 5.5 mmol/l target. (I'll have more to say on type of carbs later in the chapter.)

On the other hand, a very high BG of 14.5 mmol/l will need a bit of bolus insulin before a 30-minute bike ride, as the exercise alone will only drop me to around 11 mmol/l, which is still higher than my goal. I'd take 1.5 units in that scenario, a 75% reduction over my typical correction for a BG of 14.5 mmol/l.

It's impossible to nail this guessing game every time, but asking these three questions - what is the starting destination, ending destination, and road conditions – has brought a lot more BG predictability and less frustration to my daily exercise routine. You will have different insulin dose changes and eating approaches, though the questions discussed above will still apply.

At the end of this chapter, I've included three detailed examples that apply these questions step-by-step, along with a summary of exactly how I deal with BGs for different activities.

WHAT HELPS ME

DEVELOP MY OWN PERSONAL GUIDELINES BY EXERCISING WITH A SLIGHTLY HIGH STARTING BG (11 MMOL/L), BUT NO FOOD OR INSULIN WITHIN THE PAST FEW HOURS.

Morning exercise works well, since there are fewer variables in play. The goal is to answer the question, "How much does *activity alone* (no food or bolus insulin influence) change my BG?" Repeating this experiment a few times is important, since the BG change can vary from day to day. Once you have some BG estimates, exercise planning becomes a lot easier.

WEAR CGM DURING EXERCISE TO BETTER ANSWER THESE QUESTIONS, RECEIVE FEEDBACK, AND INFORM SMALL CHANGES ON THE FLY (E.G., EAT SOMETHING NOW?).

I often don't feel low symptoms during exercise, something CGM also helps with.

EXERCISE HAS UNPREDICTABLE EFFECTS ON BG, PARTICULARLY WHEN USING INSULIN. DON'T EXPECT PERFECTION.

For me, BG changes during exercise seem to differ based on:

- **TIME** | I often see a smaller BG drop in the morning, when I tend to be more insulin resistant. This can be an advantage when struggling with exercise-related lows, particularly because there are less food and insulin factors to deal with early in the morning.
- **INTENSITY** | Very high intensity exercise can increase OR decrease blood sugar. It's hard to predict, so for safety, my default assumption is a BG drop. Those who compete may also see differences between practice (BG drops) and game day (BG increases from adrenaline).
- **WHAT I ATE** | Eating some protein and fat before activity often keeps my BG more stable than just eating some carbs alone. My food intake for the previous 12 hours also sometimes matters: if I've eaten a lot of food on a particular day, I might see steadier BGs than on a day when I've barely eaten anything.

IMPORTANT NOTE: CHANGES IN PUMP BASAL INSULIN TAKE ABOUT 60-90 MINUTES TO HAVE A MEANINGFUL IMPACT ON BG, AND CAN STILL IMPACT BG THREE OR MORE HOURS LATER.

I used to suspend my insulin pump instead of eating right before basketball practice, which was completely useless: I would go low during exercise and high after exercise. Pump basal insulin changes need to come *at least one hour* before the desired impact on BG. For me, a small amount of food before exercise is a better option for preventing during-exercise lows, since it requires less planning. If food is eaten within 20 minutes of starting activity, I choose carbs that raise BG quickly. (See the Landmine later in this chapter.)

FOR THOSE ON INJECTIONS, MY FRIENDS WITH DIABETES RECOMMEND PREDICTING ACTIVITY LEVELS AND ADJUSTING BASAL INSULIN DOSES AHEAD OF TIME.

For instance, an inactive day may need more basal in the morning, while an active day may need less basal during the day or overnight.

 Choose activities I find fun and actually want to do. Am I looking forward to exercise tomorrow?

I must constantly remind myself that I have limited time in life, meaning I should aim to spend as much of it doing things I love.

One of my Exercise Bright Spots is so simple it seems silly to say: choose activities I find fun! I know I've found the right activity when I answer "YES" to the question, "Am I looking forward to exercising tomorrow?"

Exercise should be enjoyable, and I firmly believe there is an activity and schedule out there for every person. I know people that love running on a treadmill before work, while others swear by rock climbing at the gym after work, or biking 50 miles before 9 am, or simply going on a walk as an afternoon break.

My Exercise "Fun" ≠ Your Exercise "Fun"

For me, the key to making exercise fun has been finding the right combination of traits that appeal to my personality and fit within my life constraints (schedule, weather, location, physical ability):

- **INDIVIDUAL VS. GROUP OR TEAM** | Do I like to be alone (clear my head) or with other people (social) during exercise?
- **INSIDE VS. OUTSIDE** | Do I love the outdoors? Or do I live in a place where outdoor exercise is very difficult?
- **ENDURANCE (LONG, STEADY) VS. EXPLOSIVE (SHORT, INTENSE)** | Do I enjoy the challenge of short bursts of activity or the Zen state of longer but less intense exercise?
- **ROUTINE VS. VARIETY** | Do I want my exercise to be predictable (e.g., the same running loop) or different every time (e.g., a class that always changes)?

I've experimented with all sorts of combinations, and what I consider "FUN" changes all the time. Being outside is something I value far more than ever before: cycling in a local park, walking my dog around the neighborhood in the mornings, and hiking on weekends. I also love variety and challenge, which makes strength training and high-intensity exercise appealing.

Cherise Shockley, one of my friends with diabetes and founder of the weekly Twitter chat #DSMA, summarized this Bright Spot beautifully in a recent conversation with me:

"When you've found the best exercise for you, you will know. You will be mad when you miss it, sad when life gets in the way, cry when it is too hard to do, and love when you walk out the door. My brother told me to stop

looking at exercise as a chore and look at it as a lifestyle. Once you can look at exercise as a need-to-do versus a want-to-do, it will become a way of life."

CONSTANTLY EXPERIMENT WITH NEW ACTIVITIES AND BE WILLING TO CHANGE MY ROUTINE.

How could I make exercise something I look forward to and a highlight of my day?

IF EXERCISE BECOMES BORING, FIND WAYS TO MIX IT UP:

What could I change to make this more fun or different? What activity have I always thought about trying but never made the jump?

SIGN UP FOR A DIABETES-RELATED WALK, RUN, OR RIDE TO RAISE MONEY FOR RESEARCH.

Connecting my effort to a larger purpose adds motivation on those days when I feel too tired to train.

REGISTER AND PAY FOR AN EXERCISE EVENT THAT FEELS SLIGHTLY AMBITIOUS.

This could be anything from a local 5K to a marathon, or a 15-mile fun bike ride to a 100-mile century. A prepaid commitment can fuel the desire to get out and move, especially when I'm falling off the wagon on my normal exercise routine. Of course, use caution and choose carefully - if the event is too overwhelming and I don't have a realistic training plan, it's easy to blow it off when the day arrives.

Find the right before-exercise glucose target, and learn how many carbs are needed to raise BG to that target

Exercise can change BG rapidly - I've seen drops of 1 mmol/l in six minutes, meaning a 5 mmol/l drop in BG in just 30 minutes. This is what makes exercise so powerful for reducing a high BG but also risky for experiencing lows.

Starting activity at a higher blood glucose is one of my Bright Spots for avoiding lows *during* exercise. A target of 8 mmol/l or slightly above (depending on the activity) provides a nice buffer to avoid lows. I've personally found that anything over 11 mmol/l makes me feel sluggish, grumpy, and generally leaves me with a high BG after exercising.

My target varies depending on the activity I'm doing and how long I plan to do it. For instance, a 90-minute bike ride usually needs a starting glucose of around 9 mmol/l, while a 30-minute walk is better served with a starting value of around 7 mmol/l.

It definitely helps to know how much I need to eat at what time to raise my glucose to my desired pre-exercise target. For example, I know one glucose tab (4 grams of carbs) increases my BG by around 1 mmol/l within about 10 minutes. If I'm at 3.5 mmol/l, I know I need four tabs just before exercise to get up to 7.5 mmol/l so that I can exercise for an hour safely. A piece of fruit also works well about 30 minutes before starting exercise; I usually go with an apple.

CGM trend information is valuable too – a before-exercise BG of 8 mmol/l and two down arrows will require food before a one-hour bike ride, while an 8 mmol/l with two up arrows likely won't.

WHAT HELPS ME

FIGURE OUT:
__ (amount of food) raises my BG by ___ mmol/l within ___ minutes.

<u>1 small apple</u> raises my BG by <u>4 mmol/l</u> within <u>30 minutes</u>.
<u>1 glucose tablet</u> raises my BG by <u>1 mmol/l</u> within <u>15 minutes</u>.

TRY DIFFERENT BEFORE-EXERCISE TARGETS TO FIND OUT WHAT WORKS (E.G., 8, 10, 11 MMOL/L).

Checking BG before and after exercise is the best way to figure out an ideal target. The level may vary based on the:

- **TYPE OF EXERCISE** | A one-hour walk might need a target of 7, while running might need a target of 10 mmol/l.
- **LENGTH OF EXERCISE** | A higher target is usually needed for longer activities.
- **TIME OF DAY** | I typically see less of a BG drop in the morning.
- **LEVEL OF FITNESS** | Highly fit athletes may need a lower target, since activity may not change BG as much.

IF I'M CLOSE TO STARTING EXERCISE AND MY BG IS TOO LOW (E.G., 3 MMOL/L), I EAT OR DRINK SOMETHING WITH CARBS THAT RAISE BLOOD GLUCOSE QUICKLY.

Read more on this in the "Eating too close to exercise" Landmine. Although it may be frustrating, it's critical to wait until BG has increased to a safe level before starting any activity.

Eliminate the barriers to exercise with home workouts and exercise apps

Activity can easily take a back seat when time is crunched. The biggest exercise efficiency Bright Spot I've discovered is the home workout. It shortcuts precious time spent commuting to the gym, but it allows me to still break a sweat.

Smartphone apps and a few exercise tools offer a truly *endless* range of workouts and challenges - different motions, repetition ranges, ordering, and timing. Though I have nowhere near the variety a fully equipped gym offers, I can generally get 80% of the workout quality of a gym with 5% of the cost *in my own home* in less time.

I own a small crate of home exercise equipment, which paid for itself in a couple months of avoided gym membership. I even picked up some at a garage sale!

- **KETTLEBELLS ($10-$50)** are great for two-handed swings, squats, rows, and presses.
- **A PULL-UP BAR ($25)** that hangs on the doorframe.
- **A WEIGHTED VEST ($30)** that makes walking and pushups more difficult.
- **RESISTANCE BANDS ($15)** for shoulder exercises, crunches, and chest presses.
- **DUMBBELLS ($5-$30)** that help for working out smaller muscle groups, like arms and shoulders.
- **A YOGA MAT ($20)** for stretching.

Home workouts are also easier than ever with the help of smartphone, tablet, and watch apps. I love that the barriers to trying apps are low ($0-$5) - if it doesn't work for me, I can always delete it. No equipment is needed (bodyweight only) for most of the apps out there, and the spectrum of offerings is striking: strength training, martial arts, yoga, etc.

Here are some of the apps I've found useful:

- **7 MINUTE WORKOUT (7minuteworkout.jnj.com)** | Bodyweight workouts that are extremely efficient, highly varied, and based on my skill level and energy that day. The gorgeous design and on-screen instruction are some of the best I've seen.
- **YOGA STUDIO (yogastudioapp.com)** | Remarkable app for doing yoga and stretching at home, no equipment or experience needed.
- **MYWOD (dreamworkshopapps.com/mywod)** | Great timers for doing home workouts without any equipment; I use the tabata timers frequently.
- **OTHER POPULAR WORKOUT APPS** that don't require equipment include Fitness Buddy, Full Fitness, and Fitstar. New apps pop up every day, so I'm always visiting the app store and experimenting with what comes out.

WHAT HELPS ME

CONSTANTLY STRIVE TO REDUCE BARRIERS TO EXERCISE, INCLUDING HOME WORKOUTS, WALKING, RUNNING, CYCLING, ETC.

For me, the advantages of home exercise (convenience, time savings, consistent routine, privacy) dramatically outweigh the downsides (slightly less variety, lower intensity, no people around).

LOOK AT THE HIGHEST RANKED, MOST POPULAR, AND NEWEST FITNESS APPS IN THE GOOGLE PLAY (ANDROID) OR APPLE APP STORES AND TRY A FEW.

Most are free or less than a cup of coffee and could actually change my life.

USE INTERVALS TO ALTERNATE BURSTS OF ACTIVITY WITH SHORT REST PERIODS.

This approach crams more work into less time, and studies show it can provide similar fitness benefits as much longer exercise sessions.[31]

1 **TABATA** | 20 seconds of one exercise and 10 seconds rest, repeated 8 times = 4 minutes (one interval). A good option is to alternate between different exercises: 20 seconds of pushups, 10 seconds of rest, 20 seconds of bodyweight squats, 10 seconds of rest, repeat 4 times. I often invent workouts with tabatas that choose from different exercises: pushups, bodyweight squats, pull-ups, planks, jumping jacks, kettlebell swings, etc.

2 **EFFORT/REST IN A 1:2 RATIO** | Do a maximum effort of _____ (running, walking, biking, jumping jacks, squats) for 30 seconds; rest for 60 seconds. Repeat 4-6 times. Other options are 20 seconds and 40 seconds or 1 minute and 2 minutes.

Track activity with a device or an app to add motivation and friendly competition

Like calories in food and sugar in my blood, there's an invisible quality to activity – it's hard to know how active I am unless I actually measure it.

Activity tracking is one of my exercise Bright Spots for three reasons: I'm motivated by data, I love achieving things (even if they are arbitrary), and I enjoy a challenge.

I wear a tracker on my wrist every single day and aim for 10,000 steps – even if I can't get a real "workout" in, I know that hitting that goal is enough to meet recommended levels of daily activity. Over the past year, I've logged 4.6 million steps (over 12,000 per day), far more than if I hadn't tracked my activity.

Trackers have a reputation for ending up in drawers, but I'm addicted for a few reasons:

1   **Activity tracking changes my behavior and makes me more active** - the immediate feedback lets me know *in the moment* exactly how I'm doing. The number of steps on my wrist is an objective measurement of just how active I am – and as a result, I can quickly change my behavior when I'm falling short. When I visit my family (suburbs of Phoenix), I must force myself to go for neighborhood walks throughout the day, because so little activity is required to function in a city that revolves around cars. While traveling, I often pace up and down airplane aisles, through airports, and take the stairs up to my hotel room.

No Activity Tracking = No Clue How Much I'm Moving

2   **A single actionable goal.** I shoot for 10,000 steps every day – it's one number, and I either hit it or I don't. By contrast, I find that most exercise targets are confusingly worded (e.g., what constitutes "moderate" or "vigorous" activity?) and rely too much on manually

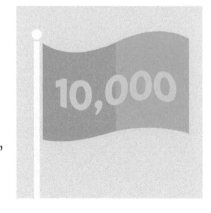

tracking time (e.g., 150 minutes per week). When it's 8 pm and I see that I'm at 9,500 steps, I'll often go for a quick walk or pace around the house to get over 10,000 steps. Does that make me weird? Maybe. But for me, having a clear line in the sand makes a big difference.

3 **Non-judgmental, motivating feedback.** While blood sugar numbers can easily feel like a judgment – "14.7 mmol/l? Ugh, what a fail!" – activity data feels very objective: "Okay – I've walked 2,500 steps today." Instead of feeling guilty or bad

about myself, usually I just feel motivated to be more active. Activity trackers also encourage with badges or salutes for reaching certain milestones (e.g., "You're almost there!" or "You've walked the length of Japan since you joined!"), plus weekly progress reports.

4 **A sense of progress over time.** Apps like Strava, Fitbit, and many others make it easy to view my activity levels over the course of a year, which build a sense of progress, momentum, and motivation. When it's December 15 and I'm 200 miles short of 2,000 cycling miles for the year, I'm more motivated to go ride.

USE AN ACTIVITY TRACKING DEVICE - IT HAS DRAMATICALLY CHANGED MY BEHAVIOR FOR THE BETTER.

The number of options increases every day, so here are a few ways to choose:

- Do any friends or family members use a particular brand? Devices like Fitbit allow you to have "friends," which definitely adds to the challenge and motivation.
- Consider other features in a device beyond activity tracking. Some devices excel at activity tracking alone, while more fully featured smartwatches can offer other benefits too (viewing CGM data on the wrist, using other apps, etc.). Both have pros and cons, and I encourage reading reviews before deciding.
- If cost is a concern, a cheaper device still works great. Less expensive trackers usually still sync to phones ($20-$75) and offer most of the exercise benefits of higher-end fancy products.
- Ask your employer for discounts - large companies often have wellness programs to give employees tracking devices.

USE THE APPLE HEALTH APP (IPHONE), GOOGLE FIT (ANDROID), OR SIMILAR APPS TO TRACK STEPS AUTOMATICALLY AND FOR FREE.

The downsides are these apps don't have as much of a social and gamification component, and you must be carrying your phone with you.

Store treatments for low BGs everywhere in my life (glucose tabs), and always carry them during exercise

There's only one thing worse than having a low during exercise: having no food on hand to treat it.

This happened to me frequently until I uncovered the core problem: I can't rely on my brain to remind me to bring low supplies; I have to outsource my memory to the environment.

My Bright Spot solution was simple:

Store tubes of glucose tablets and Smarties everywhere in my life. There are some in my bike helmet, a couple next to my bike clothes, tons in my backpack, and several next to the front door where I put my keys. I order these in bulk online, so I always have plenty around.

I rarely ever forget my low supplies now, since my environment pretty much guarantees I'll remember. The only thing I must do is order more tabs when I start to run out. Luckily, this too is easier to recall, since seeing empty tubes everywhere serves as the reorder reminder.

One other decision bias relates to this Bright Spot: "Nah, I won't go low. My BG is 10.3 mmol/l, and I'm only going out for 20 minutes." I've come to regret this logic so often that I now use a black-and-white rule: **I must ALWAYS bring low supplies with me, no matter what my starting BG is.** Nothing is more annoying than being 30 minutes into a bike ride and having to stop at a gas station and spend $5 to treat a low with junk food.

FIND A PORTABLE HYPOGLYCEMIA TREATMENT AND STORE IT WITH EXERCISE GEAR, NEAR THE FRONT DOOR, ETC.

Outsource the "need to remember" to the environment. A great book, *The Organized Mind: Thinking Straight in the Age of Information Overload* by Dr. Daniel Levitin, shares some of this research.

THE LOW TREATMENT DOESN'T HAVE TO BE GLUCOSE TABLETS OR SMARTIES, BUT IT IDEALLY SHOULD BE SMALL, EASY TO CHANGE THE QUANTITY, AND ABLE TO FIT IN A SMALL CONTAINER OR ZIPLOC BAG.

As noted in the food chapter, hard candy, gummy bears, jelly beans, and mini juice boxes can also work.

NEVER LEAVE HOME WITHOUT LOW SUPPLIES AND BRING MORE THAN I THINK I NEED, even if BG is high right before starting. I never know what will happen.

 Reduce bolus insulin based on activity type (e.g., -75% for endurance exercise, -30% before walking, no change for strength training)

Activity can add to the effects of insulin, meaning a bolus of 1 unit before a ride might actually lower my BG like a 2- or 4-unit bolus. It's easy to forget this when I'm pressed for time and skipping the diabetes math I'm supposed to be doing. The result, of course, is an annoying (and potentially very dangerous) low during an activity.

Significantly reducing bolus insulin before and during activity helps fight off hypoglycemia and keep BGs in range. This Bright Spot sounds so obvious, but no one ever explained it to me after I was first diagnosed.

For a bike ride or other endurance activity, I use a 75% reduction in bolus insulin for food or a correction. That means if I need to take 4 units to bring my glucose to my pre-exercise target, I'll instead take one unit. I apply the same logic if I'm eating carbs during activity and above my BG target – a 2-unit food bolus becomes 0.5 units. I find walking needs a 30% bolus reduction, while strength training requires no change at all.

I try to vary this reduction based on the circumstances I'm facing – a short walk of 20 minutes when my BG is 12 mmol/l will need the full bolus dose (no reduction), while a 90-minute uphill hike when I'm starting at 4 mmol/l will need at least 30 grams of carbs and no bolus at all. As I said earlier, this comes back to the starting and ending destination BG and the road conditions I'm facing that day.

Exercise also makes the body more sensitive to insulin *after* activity is over, an effect that can last for half a day or longer. For a post-exercise meal requiring 3 units, I sometimes bolus only 2 units. It all depends on how intense my activity was, what my BG is, and what I'm eating. Overnight lows are also more common following exercise, meaning a basal insulin reduction may be needed too. My basal insulin needs and exercise habits tend to change little from day to day, but I know some people that do need big changes after exercise (e.g., a 50% reduction overnight). Like other Bright Spots in this book, glucose monitoring and careful experimentation are key for finding what works for you.

WHAT HELPS ME

TAKE EXTRA CAUTION WITH BOLUS INSULIN BEFORE, DURING, AND AFTER EXERCISE.

Activity adds to the glucose-lowering effects of insulin, meaning smaller bolus doses can help avoid hypoglycemia.

TRY DIFFERENT INSULIN REDUCTIONS BASED ON THE CIRCUMSTANCES.

When I have a higher risk of going low (more intense activity, longer activity, less food, lower starting BG), I take even less insulin than normal.

CHECK BG OVERNIGHT (OR WEAR CGM) AFTER INTENSE PHYSICAL ACTIVITY.

The improvement in insulin sensitivity after exercise can last for over 12 hours.

 ## Listen to podcasts, audiobooks, or watch something entertaining during exercise

Who says exercise has to be a sufferfest?

One of my favorite Bright Spots is to use exercise for entertainment or a learning opportunity: watching a show or video, listening to audiobooks, podcasts, or TED talks. I'm constantly amazed by the goldmine of excellent, free content that expands every day.

Audio is also well suited to most activities, and it helps distract my mind and add novelty into my exercise routine.

My former *diaTribe* colleague Alasdair Wilkins lost 100 pounds in a year, mostly from one big change: one hour a day of uphill treadmill walking while watching Netflix.[32] Of course, he was also relentlessly committed and made other lifestyle changes too, but making exercise a positive thing (a source of entertainment) was a huge factor in his success.

WHAT HELPS ME

ADD ENTERTAINMENT AND LEARNING TO EXERCISE:

Listen to podcasts. There has never been a time in history with more superb, free content. Some of my favorites are the Tim Ferriss Show, NPR's How I Built This and TED Radio Hour, Tony Robbins' podcast, Serial, and Malcolm Gladwell's Revisionist History. Podcasts are an exploding medium, and there is literally one on every topic imaginable.

    · **HOW DO I DOWNLOAD A PODCAST?** | If you have an Apple device (iPhone, iPod, iPad), use the Podcasts app – it should be preinstalled on your device or can be downloaded from the App Store. If you have an Android device, download the Stitcher app from the Google Play store. Once you have one of these apps, you can subscribe to different podcasts and download episodes.

FIND BOOKS I'VE BEEN "PLANNING TO READ" FOR AGES AND LISTEN TO THEM ON AUDIO.

The Overdrive app is spectacular if you have a library card, as it allows free borrowing of audiobooks and eBooks from your local library. Audible also offers a big library of audiobooks and a monthly plan.

LISTEN TO TED TALKS DURING EXERCISE (TED.COM OR APP ON ANDROID & APPLE DEVICES).

I love learning more than most things in life, which makes TED talks a real treat.

 Schedule activity: "I lift weights on Monday, Wednesday, and Friday mornings. I ride my bike on Tuesday, Thursday, and Sunday afternoons."

"The key is not to prioritize what's on your schedule, but to schedule your priorities."

STEPHEN COVEY

In his spectacular book, *The 7 Habits of Highly Effective People*, the great time management thinker Stephen Covey classifies activities into urgent versus non-urgent and important versus non-important.[33] The most difficult category, he says, are "important" activities that are "not urgent."

That is exactly where exercise falls.

Covey argues that the best way to accomplish these activities is to schedule them; otherwise, all the urgent activities will fill up the day.

I couldn't agree more. Exercising on a schedule (even a rough subconscious one) has been a Bright Spot for me in the last few years.

I've tried a few different approaches, but here's what has stuck:

- **WEIGHT EXERCISES AT HOME** | Monday, Wednesday, and Friday mornings for 15-30 minutes before work.
- **BIKE RIDES** | Tuesday and Thursday afternoons for 45-60 minutes and one longer ride on Saturday or Sunday.

In my dream world, I would exercise in the morning before work every single day - it's a terrific insulin-free way to correct a high BG, improves my daytime blood sugars, makes overnight hypoglycemia far less likely, clears my head, and starts the day with a win. But morning rides just don't happen on many days, since I often go to bed too late and wake up with little free time or a lot of grogginess. I'm a night owl that aspires to be a morning person.

As a workaround, I've tailored my schedule based on my preferred activities, my free time on different days of the week, and my AM versus PM tendencies. I can almost always find 15 minutes in the morning to do a home workout before I start the workday, which is why I strength train before work at home three times a week. Since weekday morning bike rides just don't seem to happen, I've changed my expectations and my schedule: "I will ride my bike as an *afternoon* work break."

This subtle change has actually made a huge psychological difference. When I *expected* morning rides and didn't complete them, I felt like a failure and stressed about getting my exercise in all day. Now that I *plan* on afternoon rides as part of my schedule, I've eliminated these negative feelings.

There are still days when I can't find any time to break a sweat, but having this rough schedule has helped enormously. And when I find myself saying, "There isn't enough time to exercise," I just remember: even the busiest people on the planet find time to exercise.

WHAT HELPS ME

FIND WAYS TO *SCHEDULE* EXERCISE.

This can be subconscious or actually on the calendar, like going to a class or meeting up with a friend. Signing up for an event can also work well, since it focuses the mind and can help make exercise a bigger priority.

EXPERIMENT WITH DIFFERENT EXERCISE SCHEDULES, including time of day (morning versus afternoon versus evening) and days of the week (weekdays versus weekends). What schedule brings the highest likelihood I will exercise and enjoy it?

BE OBJECTIVE AND CHANGE MY EXPECTATIONS WHEN EXERCISE ISN'T HAPPENING ON MY PLANNED SCHEDULE.

Am I being realistic about what I can do? What else can I try?

Accountability to an exercise partner, class, or club

Companionship makes an enormous difference during exercise – the time flies and activities feel so much more enjoyable. I'm less likely to blow off exercise if I've arranged to do a bike ride with a friend or go to the gym with my brother. Some of my friends swear by exercise classes, which can address many challenges: (i) "I don't know what to do"; (ii) "I don't have the motivation to exercise on my own"; and (iii) "Exercise never makes it on my schedule."

New activities are also much easier to *start* with a partner, especially one who knows the ropes. In college, I started lifting weights because my roommate was a bodybuilder - he patiently taught my weak 18-year-old self how to lift weights properly, advice that has stuck ever since. I enjoy activities much more when I learn from the beginning how to do them well.

But with a busy professional life, I find myself caught between two opposing forces: accountability to an exercise partner or scheduled class versus freedom and autonomy to fit exercise in on *my* schedule. I generally exercise solo on time-crunched weekdays, and try to find a loved one or friend to join me for activity on weekends. In my ideal world, however, I would always have someone with me during exercise.

A partner can transform an activity into a highlight of my day - not just one more thing on the to-do list.

WHAT HELPS ME

FIND SOMEONE AT A SIMILAR SKILL LEVEL (OR AT LEAST SOMEONE WILLING TO COACH ME). Nothing is worse than feeling over my head!

BE ACCOUNTABLE TO SOMEONE WHEN TRYING *NEW* ACTIVITIES. This could be a loved one, a friend, a trainer, etc.

TRY EXERCISE CLASSES OR JOIN A LOCAL EXERCISE CLUB (E.G., RUNNING, CYCLING), especially when solo exercise is hard to sustain. Online sites like **meetup.com** and local sports stores are great places to look for groups.

TAKE ADVANTAGE OF SOCIAL ACTIVITY TRACKING APPS LIKE STRAVA, FITBIT, AND OTHERS.

I "follow" my friends, give them encouragement, and challenge them. This might sound like it could be cutthroat or competitive, but I've found it to be the exact opposite. Even the language used – "Cheer" on Fitbit and "Kudos" on Strava speaks to the positive atmosphere that these apps seek to foster. According to Fitbit's Amy McDonough, each extra "friend" on the platform increases activity by 750 steps per day.

Adopt a dog: I MUST move!

After publishing some *diaTribe* columns on exercise, a few readers wrote me with their own exercise Bright Spot: get a dog. I always thought this was cute and clever, but didn't really take it seriously.

Consider me converted.

One of the questions on the adoption paperwork for our miniature schnauzer, Sencha*, was:

"What is your plan for daily exercise?"

Then they quiz you on it before you can take the dog home.

Getting a dog is a big responsibility, and the tradeoff is not worth it for everyone. But as an exercise Bright Spot, Sencha immediately builds extra activity into my day – I have to walk every morning and evening, which helps with BGs during the toughest two times of day. And even on my worst days with diabetes, Sencha still greets me with a wagging tail when I walk in the door. In other words, dogs are an Exercise and Mindset Bright Spot all in one package!

For some people, dogs are transformative. Watch this remarkable video (**https://youtu.be/Rm0qYRWQpZI**) – it tears me up every time! – about Eric and his adopted shelter dog, Peety. Eric had type 2 diabetes and lost a remarkable 140 pounds after adopting Peety. Eric's whole mindset changed, he took up running, and he finally had the accountability to make big changes in his life. I love his ending quote: "Did I rescue him or did he rescue me?"

---

* *The name Sencha comes from our favorite Japanese green tea.*

MY EXERCISE LANDMINES

 "All or nothing" mentality: "Well, I don't have an hour, so I can't exercise"

I've been an active person for as long as I can remember, which can bring a dark side: thinking of "exercise" with an intense, all-or-nothing, I-must-break-a-sweat-and-be-exhausted frame of reference.

The proliferation of gyms, high intensity exercise classes, late night TV advertisements, and gear has upped the ante for what qualifies as "exercise."

Unfortunately, this mindset is a Landmine for those days when time is running thin: "I don't have an hour of free time, so I can't possibly exercise today." It's a lame and illogical excuse, and I do it *all the time.*

A better way to think of exercise is:

"Five minutes of activity beats zero minutes."

This liberating reframe makes the bar more realistic. The comparator for exercise is not what I see world-class athletes doing on YouTube; it's what I'm most likely to do on my packed days - nothing at all. Can I do slightly more than nothing at all? Yes, even if it's a 10-minute walk on a lunch break.

I'm most reminded of this challenge when I go to diabetes conferences, where my schedule is usually booked solid from early in the morning to late at night. There is so much to do at a conference that exercise seems completely out of the question, and often, doesn't even cross my mind. When I remember that "five minutes of activity beats zero minutes," I always come up with something: 50 jumping jacks in the hotel room, hopping on the bike in the gym for a six-minute interval, 25 bodyweight squats, or even taking the stairs up to my hotel room.

Exercise is also typically positioned as a "do it to live longer" kind of activity. But when things are busy today, it's hard to prioritize the long game, and very easy to make "I don't have time" excuses.

As I mentioned in the Mindset chapter, long-term motivators work for some people some of the time, but I also try to focus on short-term reasons to do something today. For exercise, the WHY is all the terrific immediate wins:

- Reduces my BG (most of the time).
- Cuts my insulin needs and improves my insulin sensitivity.
- Lifts my mood, improves my relationships and positivity, and reduces my stress levels, which in turn helps my BGs.
- Increases my productivity.
- Helps me sleep better, which also helps next-day BGs.
- Helps me generate new ideas.

Reframing the reward from exercise - something that benefits me immediately - boosts the benefit of doing it, and helps overcome the blow-it-off tendency when I'm tired, stressed, and feeling overwhelmed. An hour invested in exercise will actually make me more productive at my job. From that perspective, exercise isn't an "I'll do it if I have time" kind of activity, but a necessity in my daily schedule that is no different from charging my laptop or brushing my teeth.

WHAT HELPS ME

"EXERCISE" DOES NOT AUTOMATICALLY MEAN 60 MINUTES OF BREAKING A SWEAT TO EXHAUSTION.

When time is of the essence, "Five minutes of activity beats zero minutes."

CONSISTENCY CAN BE MORE IMPORTANT THAN QUALITY, ESPECIALLY IF LIFE IS BUSY.

I benefit more from 10 minutes of exercise five days per week versus one 50-minute session.

REFRAME THE REWARDS FROM EXERCISE TO SHORT-TERM BENEFITS.

How does moving my body benefit me immediately?

 ## Eating too close to starting exercise: low BG during activity, high BG after activity

Eating before exercise is a great way to start at a higher glucose target (e.g., 9 mmol/l) and prevent a low. However, exercise also slows down digestion, creating a timing problem: if I eat too close to starting my exercise, the glucose might not get into my blood until after the activity is over. That leads to a double Landmine of going low during exercise (food has not been absorbed), and then high after exercise. Gah!

The picture below shows exactly what this Landmine looks like – I ate an apple too close to starting exercise (5:05 pm), saw a BG drop during exercise (5:15-6:15 pm), and then the apple hit my system and rapidly increased my BG after I finished (6:45–8 pm). This snack was supposed to raise BG to my 9 mmol/l target before starting exercise, but I completely messed up the timing.

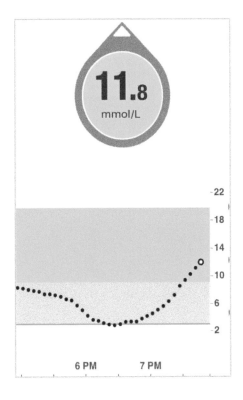

While the solution is obvious – don't eat too close to exercise – the application can be tricky. Foods differ markedly in their ability to increase blood sugar quickly. A sandwich on whole grain bread might not peak my BG for 30 minutes or more (especially if it has some fat, like cheese or avocado), while a few glucose tablets usually take 5–10 minutes.

I do best when I vary what I eat based on my timing. If my BG is at 5.5 mmol/l and I'm going to ride my bike in 10 minutes, I need something like glucose tabs. If I have 30 minutes, I might eat an apple instead. As I discussed earlier in the chapter, it's helpful to precisely adjust the amount carbs based on my current BG and pre-exercise target.

KEEP A FOOD, BG, AND EXERCISE DIARY FOR A WEEK OR TWO.

I've found it helpful for experimenting with different pre-exercise foods, amounts of food, and timing strategies - when and what do I need to eat to increase my BG before exercise, not spike it too much, and not have food hang around after my activity? Diabetes apps like mySugr, note-taking apps like Evernote, or even pen and paper can help with better decision making.

IF MY BG IS UNDER 5.5 MMOL/L CLOSE TO STARTING MY EXERCISE (within 30 minutes), opt for carbs that increase BG rapidly and bring me up to my pre-exercise glucose target.

 Overeating after exercise

After a long or particularly tiring workout, it's easy to come home and gobble up the fridge. I can easily convince myself that I've "earned" a big meal or junk food I wouldn't normally eat, particularly when I get home after 48 miles of riding and a BG of 3.4 mmol/l. This always results in a Landmine I come to regret: high BGs for hours after my post-exercise food fest.

There are several tactics I use to avoid this trap:

 Instead of going into snack-attack mode, eat a real meal after exercise: high in protein, fat, and fiber. For example, a veggie three-egg omelet, a big salad with chicken and nuts, or a low-carb wrap with tuna. I find these low-carb meals don't require a bolus after any exercise session that made me sweat.

② **If ending exercise in hypoglycemia, use my go-to, quantity limited treatment for lows** *first:* glucose tabs, a small apple, Smarties, etc. I get into trouble when I use a low BG after exercise as an excuse to overeat too much food. The hypoglycemia binge is hard to stop and difficult to carb count in the moment.

③ **Find a routine that helps me finish exercise comfortably in-range (5.5-8 mmol/l).** Ending at 6.5 mmol/l instead of 3 mmol/l makes a huge difference for my post-activity hunger. See the Bright Spots earlier in this chapter for some ideas, especially starting at a higher target BG.

④ **Drink a lot more water during and after exercise.** Often I'm mistaking hunger for thirst when I get home from a workout. Hydrating during and after activity reduces the ravenous feelings and subsequent food spree. I often use electrolyte tablets or a lime or lemon to flavor my water and ensure I drink enough. A big pot of tea also fills me up right after exercise, though I'm the first to admit this is strange.

⑤ **Do not view exercise like saving money** - "I get to splurge on something once I have enough in the bank!" Exercise is an ongoing commitment (a subscription to my favorite magazine), not a once-in-a-while Black Friday purchase (buying a new TV) - both may bring short-term satisfaction, but the splurge mentality is more likely to drive guilt and a BG Landmine.

Poor recovery: failing to stretch, not enough water, not enough sleep

Muscle soreness is a pesky exercise Landmine - it's annoying, often painful, and supremely de-motivating. Talk about a negative feedback loop!

The hills in San Francisco make my calves and hamstrings sore all the time, and cycling and strength training make it worse. I've discovered three reliable causes:

1. Failing to stretch consistently.
2. Not drinking enough water.
3. Too little sleep.

The solutions are pretty obvious, but they are worth some explanation.

Stretching and foam rolling have been highly effective for relieving my soreness; the hard part is remembering to do it. When I go a couple days without any stretching at all, it's a triple Landmine: more physical pain, less desire to exercise, and even an impaired mood.

I consistently failed to stretch until I stumbled on a simple, game-changing solution: do it for 10-15 minutes right before bed every single night. It's now become an automatic habit and had a huge positive impact on my soreness, all because I paired a new behavior (stretching) after a routine I already do every night (shower, brush teeth).

I'm also a big fan of foam rollers and own a ridged option to dig into hard-to-reach areas like the calves ("Rumble Roller"), plus a standard smooth one for larger muscles like the quads. I've been surprised how tightness in one muscle group like the hamstrings or glutes can lead to downstream soreness in a muscle like the calves. Now, I make sure my stretching hits the sore muscle *and* those around it.

I also experience more soreness when I forget to drink enough water, particularly when eating fewer carbohydrates and in warm months. According to expert low-carb researchers Drs. Jeff Volek and Stephen Phinney (authors of *The Art and Science of Low Carbohydrate Living*), when the human body adapts to eating fewer carbs, the kidneys excrete extra water and sodium, which can lead to several side effects (e.g., light headedness, cramps, fatigue, etc.). As a fix, they recommend purposefully adding 2,000-3,000 mg of sodium in those eating *less than 60 grams of carbs per day*; for those eating at or above that level, this prescription becomes "optional."[34] I tend to eat around 70-120 grams of carbs per day, and

therefore haven't noticed a big benefit from boosting my sodium intake. However, this link between water balance and eating fewer carbs is very real in my experience - I definitely need more water than the average person to stave off soreness. (Note: Use caution with this recommendation if you are on diuretics or have high blood pressure.)

Finally, sleep deprivation absolutely plays a role in my soreness; my legs always feel better on the weekends when I get 8-10 hours of sound sleep.

WHAT HELPS ME

MAKE STRETCHING PART OF MY BEFORE-BED ROUTINE.

The few minutes invested at 11 pm pays off the next day. It's helped to keep my foam roller and bands right near my bed, providing a visual reminder before going to sleep. I use a countdown timer to make sure I get at least 10-15 minutes of stretching in; without the objectivity of a clock, I will slack off and stretch for too little time. I often watch a TED talk or funny video too, just to make the time go by faster and pair stretching with something enjoyable.

SQUEEZE IN STRETCHING AT RANDOM TIMES OF DAY: as I brush my teeth, while watching my dog play in the park, etc. Tooth brushing is an example of what Dr. BJ Fogg calls an "anchor" –

something I do every day that I can easily stack a new behavior on top of.

DRINK MORE WATER!

Carrying a big reusable water bottle definitely reminds me to stay hydrated. It sounds silly, but investing in a nice-looking bottle that I enjoy using makes a difference too. Plus, hydration seems to help with my BG control; I run higher when I haven't had enough water to drink.

WATCH DR. KELLY STARRETT ON YOUTUBE (www.youtube. com/user/sanfranciscocrossfit)

He is a respected expert on this topic, the NYT best-selling author of *Becoming a Supple Leopard*, and has some very effective (and often unconventional) tactics. His approaches to freeing up calf tightness have helped me a lot.

 Focusing on how painful exercise feels while doing it

In the middle of an exercise session, when all I want to do is quit, it's easy to focus on the pain. "This is the worst. This is awful. I hate this. Why am I doing this?"

It's a psychological Exercise Landmine in the moment, and over time, can discourage exercise altogether. It's never easy to overcome this Landmine, but when it comes up, I try to use a bit of mental warfare.

 Remind myself that I am *voluntarily* exercising: I'm spending my free time to do this, so I might as well try to enjoy it, or at minimum, not hate it.

2   **Use body language to my advantage, especially smiling.** It sounds crazy, but more and more research suggests our body language influences our mental state. When my exercise feels painful and I just want to quit, forcing myself to smile actually helps a lot. Four-time World Ironman Champion Chrissie Wellington writes "smile" on all her water bottles as a reminder. This seems bizarre, but it works for me too - a smile as I slowly pedal up a long hill makes it more doable. (Watch Amy Cuddy's compelling TED Talk, "Your body language shapes who you are," or read *The Charisma Myth* by Olivia Fox Cabane for more on this topic.)

3   **Remember times when I've done something much harder; "I can do this!"** Some days I simply feel tired, even during a bike ride or weight workout I know I can do. A mental note that "I've done this done before" helps remind me that I will get through it this time.

4   **Be more mindful of how my feet are moving, what the scenery looks like, how I'm breathing,** or what the podcast I'm listening to is talking about. Diverting my attention to other things helps distract me from the workout.

QUESTIONS TO ASK YOURSELF

 ## Bright Spot Questions

How might you build activity into your daily routine automatically, especially walking?

Remember the last time you exercised and really enjoyed it ("That was fun!"). What was that activity? What contributed to those positive feelings?

On days when you do get to exercise, how did you make it happen? What was your schedule?

Think about times when your blood sugar stayed in range (ideally 5.5–10 mmol/l) during and after exercise:

- What did you eat? How much did you eat? When did you eat?
- What was your starting BG? What was your ending BG?
- (If applicable) How much bolus insulin did you take? When did you take it? Did you adjust your basal insulin at all?
- Can you replicate these conditions?

(If exercise is not fun) What can you change about your routine to make exercise more fun? Can you try a new activity? A different intensity? A different time of day? A different route? Entertainment during your activity? A partner to hold you accountable?

Look at the answers above. What are your Bright Spots – the things you can try to do more often? How might you encourage them?

Landmine Questions

When your blood sugar goes low (less than 4 mmol/l) or high (over 10 mmol/l) during or after exercise, what do you think caused it? For example, a starting BG that was too high or low, eating too much or too little around exercise, taking too much or too little insulin, etc. Do you have any clear patterns?

On days when you do *not* get to exercise, what happened?

What are your worst experiences with exercise? What exercise do you not enjoy but try to force anyways?

Look at the answers above. What are your Landmines – the things you can try to do less often? How might you avoid them?

HOW I DEAL WITH EXERCISE AND APPLYING THE BG QUESTIONS

HOW I DEAL WITH BGS AND EXERCISE

The following tables share the blood sugar, insulin, and exercise strategies that seem to work for me; they are not intended to be universal recommendations for everybody. By sharing them, I hope my approaches can help you come up with your own strategy in coordination with your healthcare provider. Remember that there are many factors that influence blood glucose and you may respond very differently!

CHECKLIST BEFORE STARTING ACTIVITY

☐ BG above 5.5 mmol/l? (If not, eat something!)

IDEALLY CARRY:

☐ Glucose tabs or similar for lows   ☐ CGM or BG meter

☐ My phone (in case I need help)   ☐ Water

☐ Tell someone where I'm going and for how long

☐ A medical alert bracelet (I use one from RoadID that

    includes my name, medications, and emergency contacts)

A. WALKING

Expected BG Change for Walking	Drop of 1 mmol/l in 15 minutes on flat ground Drop of 1-2 mmol/l in 15 minutes if insulin was recently taken or if walking uphill
Food	**BEFORE** | Eat 5-10 g carbs if BG is under 5 mmol/l, and more carbs if insulin was recently taken or I'm trending low. **DURING** | Glucose tabs or similar if BG goes below 5 mmol/l. Each glucose tab raises my blood sugar by about 1 mmol/l. **AFTER** | Nothing different
Insulin	**BOLUS** | A 30% reduction for a food or correction bolus if walking more than 30 minutes.

B. BIKING/RUNNING, LESS THAN 90 MINUTES

For activity less than 90 minutes, I avoid pump basal rate changes entirely and simply eat some carbs right before I start, if needed (to get my BG up to target); eat as needed during activity to maintain a glucose between 5.5-10 mmol/l; and reduce any needed correction bolus insulin by 75% during activity.

Expected BG Change for Biking	Drop of 3.5 mmol/l in 30 minutes

Food	**BEFORE** | Eat before activity to reach a target of approximately 9 mmol/l. Generally this means: • 30 grams of carbs if BG is under 4 mmol/l • 20-30 grams of carbs if BG is 4-7 mmol/l • 10-20 grams of carbs if BG is 7-9 mmol/l • No carbs if BG is over 9 mmol/l • 24 ounces of fluid (usually water or green tea) **DURING** | Glucose tabs or similar if below 5.5 mmol/l **AFTER** | Medium-sized meal with 15-30 grams of carbs, high fat, protein, and fiber
Insulin	**BOLUS** | 75% reduction in correction insulin before and during exercise (i.e., from a four-unit to a one-unit bolus). No change in bolus insulin following exercise. **PUMP BASAL** | No change

C. BIKING, MORE THAN 90 MINUTES

For the more challenging longer activities, I usually eat right before exercise, if needed (to get my BG up to target and give me some buffer); start a 50% basal reduction as I begin activity; eat as needed during activity to maintain a glucose between 5.5-10 mmol/l; and then stop the basal reduction one hour *before* I plan to finish. If my BG goes over 10 mmol/l during exercise, I take a bolus correction that is 75% smaller than normal. When I don't want to eat before activity, the 50% pump basal reduction has to start at least one hour *before* I begin. Here's what it looks like:

Expected BG Change for Biking	Drop of 3.5 mmol/l in 30 minutes
Food	**BEFORE** | Eat before activity to reach a target of approximately 9 mmol/l. Generally this means: • 30 grams of carbs if BG is under 4 mmol/l • 20–30 grams of carbs if BG is 4–7 mmol/l • 10–20 grams of carbs if BG is 7–9 mmol/l • No carbs if BG is over 9 mmol/l **DURING** | 20–30 grams of carbs per hour (glucose tabs or similar); additional carbs when trending low **AFTER** | Medium-sized meal with 30 grams of carbs, high fat, protein, and fiber
Insulin	**BOLUS** | 75% reduction in food and correction insulin before and during activity; 20% food bolus reduction after activity **PUMP BASAL** | If eating before exercise, I use a 50% reduction starting when exercise begins and ending one hour before it's over. That means for a 1–4:30 pm bike ride, I'd run a 50% basal reduction from 1–3:30 pm. If I choose not to eat before exercise, the basal reduction needs to start at 12 pm (one hour before) and run to 3:30 pm (one hour before finishing).

D. STRENGTH TRAINING

Expected BG Change	No change or a 1-2 mmol/l rise
Food	**BEFORE** | None (I usually train on an empty stomach) **DURING** | None (BG usually doesn't change or rises) **AFTER** | High protein breakfast (chia pudding, eggs, nuts, seeds)
Insulin	**BOLUS** | No change **PUMP BASAL** | No change

APPLYING THE BRIGHT SPOT QUESTIONS - THREE DETAILED EXAMPLES

Your experience and numbers will vary, but the charts on the next page show the starting destination, ending destination, and road condition exercise questions in action.

EXAMPLE 1. HIGH BG WITH NO RECENT INSULIN AND NO RECENT FOOD

1. What is my BG now?

START · · · · (**10** mmol/l)

2. How much do I expect my BG to change by the time I finish exercising?

ESTIMATED BG CHANGE FOR 30 MIN BIKE RIDE · · · · · (▼**3.5** mmol/l)

RECENT FOOD OR BOLUS INSULIN? · · · · · (None)

END · · · · (**6.5** mmol/l)

3. Any food or insulin changes now to: (i) stay in the zone of 5.5-10 mmol/l during exercise; and (ii) finish as close to 5.5 mmol/l as possible?

No food or bolus insulin needed.

With a 10 mmol/l starting BG, exercise alone (no recent bolus insulin or food) is expected to bring my BG down to around 6.5 mmol/l.

EXAMPLE 2. IN-RANGE BG WITH RECENT BOLUS INSULIN

1. What is my BG now?

START · · · · **7** *mmol/l*

2. How much do I expect my BG to change by the time I finish exercising?

ESTIMATED BG CHANGE FOR 30 MIN BIKE RIDE · · · · · ▼**3.5** *mmol/l*

RECENT FOOD OR BOLUS INSULIN? · · · · · **2** *units of bolus insulin* **60 mins** *ago.*

WHY <3.5?
Activity accelerates bolus insulin, driving BG even lower.

END · · · · **<3.5** *mmol/l*

3. Any food or insulin changes now to: (i) stay in the zone of 5.5-10 mmol/l during exercise; and (ii) finish as close to 5.5 mmol/l as possible?

Eat at least 30 grams of fast-acting carbs (glucose tabs or similar).

With a 7 mmol/l starting BG, exercise alone will likely bring me down to 3.5 mmol/l, and recent insulin will drop me further. I need to eat to cover both.

EXAMPLE 3. HIGH BG, FOOD AND INSULIN ON BOARD

1. What is my BG now?

START · · · · 14.5 *mmol/l*

2. How much do I expect my BG to change by the time I finish exercising?

ESTIMATED BG CHANGE FOR 30 MIN BIKE RIDE · · · · · ▼3.5 *mmol/l*

WHY ~9.5?

Bolus insulin tends to drop BG for 3+ hours after taking it, meaning more than half is still around 1 hour later. By contrast, carbs usually peak by 60 minutes, meaning they are mostly absorbed here. Activity will accelerate the insulin that is still working, so the net effect of food and insulin should drive my BG lower.

RECENT FOOD OR BOLUS INSULIN?

20 *grams of carbs* **60 mins** *ago.*

2 *units of bolus insulin* **60 mins** *ago.*

END · · · · ~9.5 *mmol/l*

3. Any food or insulin changes now to: (i) stay in the zone of 5.5-10 mmol/l during exercise; and (ii) finish as close to 5.5 mmol/l as possible?

Take 0.75 units of correction bolus insulin (75% less than a full dose).

Starting at 14.5 mmol/l, exercise alone will drop me to 11 mmol/l. The net effect of food and insulin will take me to ~9.5 mmol/l. This is still above my goal of 5.5 mmol/l. A bolus dose will bring me closer to target, but since it's right before exercise, I'd take a smaller-than-usual dose of 0.75 units instead of 3 units.

04

Sleep

Getting a Good Night of Rest

WHY IS SLEEP in this BOOK?

It has a strong connection to diabetes: studies repeatedly show too little sleep is associated with higher A1c and BG levels; greater insulin resistance; more hunger, calorie consumption, and carb cravings; weight gain; higher levels of depression; lower quality of life; and beyond.[35] A slew of biological changes occur with too little sleep, including higher levels of cortisol (stress), increased inflammation, and changes in hunger hormones, which can all contribute to greater insulin resistance and higher BGs.[36]

Sleep is a highly underrated diabetes tool, especially because it is changeable almost immediately: I can almost always get more sleep tonight if I make it a priority.

CHAPTER SUMMARY

 Sleep

MY BRIGHT SPOTS | p. 190

- At least 7 hours of sleep: more next-day BGs in range, less insulin, more energy, better mood, less hunger
- Overnight BGs in a tight range (4.5-8 mmol/l): early dinner, no snacking, disciplined bedtime corrections
- Glucose tablets next to my bed: no refrigerator eating, less disrupted sleep
- Limit light exposure at night, and use an app/device setting to limit blue screen light
- Invest in a better mattress and pillow and do not settle for uncomfortable sleep
- Cooler room temperature (65 degrees) and a lighter blanket
- Morning or afternoon exercise to fall asleep faster
- Phone charging in a separate room or in airplane mode starting at 10:30 pm

MY LANDMINES | p. 204

- Nighttime fear: overeating right before bed
- Too much caffeine after 2 pm
- Waking up in the morning in a completely dark room

QUESTIONS TO ASK YOURSELF | p. 209

MY SLEEP BRIGHT SPOTS

 At least 7 hours of sleep: more next-day BGs in range, less insulin, more energy, better mood, less hunger

Getting 7 or more hours of sleep per night is a Diabetes Bright Spot on many fronts:

- I see more BGs in my target range on the following day, especially after breakfast.
- I need less insulin the next day.
- I feel more energized for morning exercise.
- I'm in a better mood and less frustrated over small diabetes and life hassles.
- I make better diabetes decisions and I am more able to resist tempting foods.
- My body is less sore from exercise.

But of all the Bright Spots in this book, I most consistently fall short on this one. I've most recently averaged just under seven hours of sleep during the week, not enough for me to be at my best.

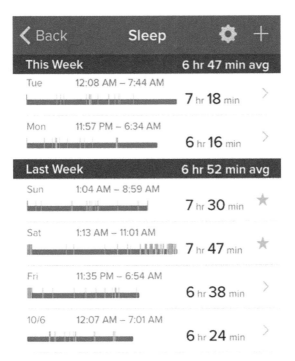

I'm a night owl and find it easy to stay up late, but I also love the idea of being a morning person. It's a bad combination!

When I do get 7 or more hours of sleep, usually one of the following helps:

- I stick to a firm get-ready-for-bed time - at 10:30 pm, I make moves to shower, brush teeth, and get into pajamas.
- I decide to wake up later the following morning, accepting the consequences of not being able to exercise or do as much before the day starts. I try to do this no more than a few times per week.
- I reel in the "achiever" in me and realize I don't have to finish whatever I'm working on tonight.
- I focus on what I will gain the next day by getting more sleep tonight: clearer thinking, happier state of mind, more productivity, more BGs in my target range, etc.

I think sleep is just as important as any other health behavior, and it is also just as difficult to change: modifying habits takes focused effort, and sometimes the tradeoffs are hard to swallow (e.g., earlier to bed means less time to spend with loved ones at night). This Bright Spot is definitely a constant work in progress for me.

WHAT HELPS ME

TRACK SLEEP WITH A DEVICE, APP, OR JOURNAL TO GET A SENSE OF HOW MUCH I'M GETTING.

Most wrist-worn activity tracking devices can now measure sleep, though a growing number of apps and bedside devices can do it too. In the past I used an app called Sleep Cycle that ran on my phone and tracked movement while sitting on the bed - it wasn't as accurate as a wrist-worn device, but it was much better than nothing. "Sleep tech" is now a hot industry and many new tracking devices are coming out that attach to the mattress or pillow or simply sit on the night stand – these are definitely worth exploring if you are not sleeping well.

HAVE A FIRM GET-READY -FOR-BED TIME (E.G., 10:30 PM) AND SET A PHONE ALARM(S) THAT GOES OFF AT THAT TIME EVERY NIGHT.

It's really easy to just shut the alarm off, so this must be paired with true commitment to get more sleep. It's actually helped me to set two alarms - a "yellow light" alarm at 9:30 pm ("Hey Adam, bedtime is coming soon") and a "red light" alarm at 10:30 pm ("Get ready for bed - now!").

ASK A LOVED ONE TO JOIN ME IN A QUEST TO SLEEP MORE.

My girlfriend and I hold each other accountable!

READ SOME OF THE RESEARCH ON SLEEP DEPRIVATION

It's terrifying to see how lack of sleep negatively impacts most things in life, and also good motivation to get to sleep earlier. If I want to be the best person I can be, I must sleep well.

 ## Overnight BGs in a tight range (4.5-8 mmol/l): early dinner, no snacking, disciplined bedtime corrections

Keeping my BG in a tight range overnight (4.5-8 mmol/l) dramatically improves my sleep quality and next-day restfulness. Nighttime highs and lows really disrupt sleep, and the more dramatic or prolonged they are, the worse I end up feeling the following morning: exhausted, grumpy, and likely to either overeat (to correct a low) or remain high for much of the next day.

What makes nighttime BGs profoundly difficult is that they are influenced by a number of factors: food during the day; dinner and nighttime snacking (size, type, timing); daytime exercise; insulin dose and timing; and more. Basal insulin requirements can also change drastically from night to night – in studies of automated insulin delivery, people with diabetes sometimes need *half as much* basal insulin on some nights and *twice as much* insulin on other nights. This makes repeatable perfection challenging!

Nighttime is also a scary time to live with diabetes - given the potential for severe hypoglycemia - so my instinct is to be ultra conservative before bed with food (eating too much) and insulin dosing (taking too little). Upcoming automated insulin delivery (artificial pancreas) systems will be a major overnight Bright Spot, but not everyone may want to or be able to use them.

When I have a Bright Spot night of BGs (4.5-8 mmol/l), there are usually some key enablers:

- I have a filling early dinner with lots of veggies, a modest portion of protein, and plenty of fluids at least three hours before bed.
- I stick to a black-and-white rule to prevent snacking - I do NOT eat after dinner unless I'm low.
- I correct lows before bed with a quantity-limited food (a small apple, glucose tabs, Smarties), eating just enough to get back to my target range.

Just as with food, glucose monitoring (ideally with CGM) is the key feedback mechanism for this Bright Spot - am I *consistently* going high or low during sleep? How does my BG usually change from pre-bed to waking up? What might be driving the pattern, particularly my food habits?

I'm careful about changing my overnight basal insulin dose from night to night, since my routine tends to vary minimally. I get into trouble when I use one isolated night of BGs (e.g., two hours spent low on Monday) and impulsively change my entire weekly basal insulin plan. This is never a good idea. My personal nighttime patterns are often inconsistent (high on Monday, low on Tuesday), and I find my eating habits are typically the biggest driver. (The obvious exception is if I have a *consistent* high or low pattern on *most* nights in a period of two weeks - then I do change my basal insulin dose.)

LOOK FOR OVERNIGHT BG PATTERNS:

Does my BG stay relatively level throughout an average night (within about 2 mmol/l from before bed to waking up), or does it consistently rise or fall from bedtime to wakeup? If BG is consistently changing on most nights, talk to your healthcare provider about your medication dose. (Insulin users can read more on this topic from Gary Scheiner at **diatribe.org/basaltesting**)

ON BRIGHT SPOT NIGHTS, WHAT COMBINATION OF FACTORS MAY HAVE CONTRIBUTED TO IN-RANGE BGS?

On the other hand, when my BG goes far out of range from pre-bed to waking up, was there an obvious driver? If this happens consistently, how might I change my eating routine or medication?

FOCUS ON FOOD – IT'S THE BIGGEST DRIVER OF MY HIGH AND LOW BG PATTERNS OVERNIGHT.

What foods and timing help keep me in range overnight, including dinner and nighttime snacks? Can I be more consistent with my evening eating? What bedtime low correction brings me back in range and keeps my BG stable overnight?

REMEMBER THAT OVERNIGHT PERFECTION IS DIFFICULT WHEN MANUALLY DOSING INSULIN.

Strive for improvement, use data to make decisions, and experiment conservatively. I'm always in learning mode and still constantly making mistakes.

USE AUTOMATED INSULIN DELIVERY OVERNIGHT, IF IT'S ACCESSIBLE TO YOU (ALSO KNOWN AS A "HYBRID CLOSED LOOP" OR "ARTIFICIAL PANCREAS").

These systems are outstanding overnight - almost every morning while wearing one, most people wake up around 5-7 mmol/l.

IF USING A PUMP IN OPEN LOOP (NO AUTOMATION), REMEMBER BASAL INSULIN CHANGES SHOULD BE MADE AT LEAST ONE HOUR BEFORE THE ACTUAL LOW OR HIGH OCCURS (i.e., a change in basal dose takes time to actually affect my BG).

 ## Glucose tablets next to my bed: no refrigerator eating, less disrupted sleep

I keep glucose tablets and Smarties next to my bed for one reason: when I wake up low at 3 am, there is an immediate, auto-pilot fix and I can go to back to sleep. This Bright Spot has improved my overnight blood sugars (no overeating-from-the-fridge-at-3:01 am) and prevented sleep disruption (no walking into the kitchen and blinding myself with light from the fridge).

There are plenty of convenient places to store hypoglycemia corrections,

including on a nightstand, on the floor next to the bed, or even in a bedside pocket on the side of the bed. I'm a fan of the latter, which slips between the mattress and bedside railing and also holds my meter and CGM.

Storing an object at the critical point of use is obvious: it's instinctive to hang house keys or put shoes by the door, have pans and oil near the stove, and put napkins and salt on the kitchen table. But in the domain of sleep and BGs, I've been shocked at how useful this has been.

 Limit light exposure at night, and use an app/device setting to limit blue screen light

I sleep best when I limit my exposure to light at night – particularly blue light from screens.

The human body undergoes chemical changes in response to less light in the evening (more sleepiness) and more light in the morning (more wakefulness). Too much light at night can make it harder to fall asleep. My Bright Spot solutions for reducing light exposure have taken several forms:

1 **Turning down the overhead lights in my apartment after dinner and relying on small lamps and night lights.** I have an old school Edison bulb (incandescent light) on the wall, plus a string of white Christmas tree lights in the living room – both provide just enough light to read, but not too much to keep me up late. My bedroom has a bedside alarm clock that doubles as a lamp with a dimmer to adjust brightness (Philips Wake-Up Light).

2 **Not using any screen within an hour of bed, or installing an app like f.lux (<u>justgetflux.com</u>) or using Night Shift mode (on newer Apple devices) to change a screen's color temperature based on time of day.** f.lux and Night Shift mode automatically reduce the amount of blue light from a screen as the sun sets, which may improve sleep. Some companies also make screen covers that limit blue light. A more disciplined option, of course, is not to look at any screens within 60 minutes of bed – I don't do a great job of that every night, but it does make a difference when I remember.

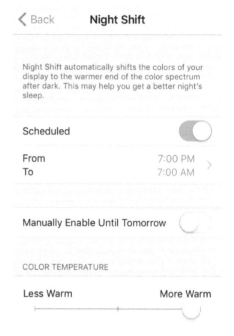

3 **Showering before bed in very low light (night light or candle).** I'm one of those strange people that showers at 11 pm: the warm water makes me sleepy and frees my mind before the day comes to a close. One thing I started doing a couple years ago was showering in near-darkness, relying on dim light only from a wall-plugin night light or a candle. Most bathrooms tend to be very bright and reflective, a poor combination right before bed.

WHAT HELPS ME

ASSESS HOW MUCH LIGHT I AM GETTING AT NIGHT, BOTH FROM LAMPS AND SCREENS.

Can I change the number or types of light I use in my living space?

REDUCE SCREEN TIME 60 MINUTES BEFORE BED, AND TRY F.LUX, NIGHTSHIFT MODE (ON NEWER APPLE DEVICES), OR A SIMILAR APP TO AUTOMATICALLY LIMIT BLUE WAVELENGTH LIGHT FROM SCREENS.

I love that these operate in the background (based on time of day) and I don't have to remember to toggle them on.

READ BEFORE BED IN LOW LIGHT, IDEALLY WITH A PHYSICAL BOOK.

This helps the mind wind down and ease into sleep. Plus, it helps me forget about my worries and all the things I have to do tomorrow.

IDENTIFY TINY SOURCES OF LIGHT IN MY BEDROOM AND COVER THEM UP.

Some experts say tiny alarm clock lights and blinking lights on powered-down devices can disrupt sleep too. Blackout curtains can help block external light streaming in from windows.

 Invest in a better mattress and pillow and do not settle for uncomfortable sleep

"An investment in sleep pays the best interest."

MY PERSONAL REMIX OFF OF BENJAMIN FRANKLIN'S EDUCATION ADVICE

I will spend nearly one-third of my life asleep.

It's an astonishing amount of time that dwarfs most other activities in life. Yet, it's so easy to just settle for average or below average in the sleep domain. For years, I slept on a cheap foam mattress and pillow. They seemed fine, and it never occurred to me that I could do much better if I did some research and spent just a little bit more money.

As I've realized what a Bright Spot night of sleep can do for my diabetes and my life, I've started to take my sleep environment more seriously. One of the best investments I've made in the past few years was buying a better mattress made by the company Casper. The mattress is cooler, more comfortable, helps me fall asleep faster, and causes less back pain in the morning. Plus, it was far less expensive than I would have guessed, and I made some money back selling my old mattress.

A new pillow makes a difference too, as I discovered after buying one from Parachute Home. To my surprise, different levels of firmness are actually recommended for back versus side versus stomach sleepers.

WHAT HELPS ME

DO NOT SETTLE FOR CRAPPY SLEEP – IF A PILLOW OR MATTRESS ISN'T GETTING THE JOB DONE, TRY SOMETHING NEW.

Companies like Casper, Parachute Home, Tuft & Needle, Leesa, and many others now offer money-back guarantees that take uncertainty out of sleep purchases (e.g., "100-night free trial"). They also typically ship mattresses for free door-to-door, and it actually comes in a reasonable-sized box.

Cooler room temperature (65 degrees) and a lighter blanket

The National Sleep Foundation reports that a cool room temperature of around 65 degrees Fahrenheit makes for the best sleep.[37] This definitely backs my own experience: I sleep far worse at other temperatures, particularly in hotter rooms. I've also found my overnight BGs stay in range more often at cooler room temperatures, while warm rooms seem to drive my BG high – and thereby, worsen life the next day (higher BGs to start the day, less energy, worse mood).

Adjusting the thermostat is not an option in my temperate San Francisco apartment, so I've taken to using a lighter blanket, a cooler mattress, and lighter sleepwear. I rarely wake up in the middle of the night sweating like I did on that heat-retaining memory foam.

WHAT HELPS ME

FIND AN OPTIMAL SLEEPING TEMPERATURE AND ALIGN MY BEDROOM ENVIRONMENT WITH THOSE PREFERENCES.

This includes room temperature, blanket type, bedtime clothing, and even type of mattress. Do I feel well rested when the room is slightly cool or slightly warm?

Morning or afternoon exercise to fall asleep faster

Nothing is worse than getting into bed and being unable to fall asleep, which only spawns frustration, worry, and further insomnia. One of my Bright Spots for falling asleep quickly is daytime exercise – the more movement I get, the easier it is to fall asleep.

I've also found exercise timing plays a role in my drowsiness. Another reason I like morning or early afternoon workouts is they tend to energize me for the day, something I wouldn't want to do at night. I generally avoid late-night exercise, as the adrenaline wakes me up and it takes me a while to wind down.

REMEMBER THE EXERCISE-SLEEP CONNECTION.

Activity can help me fall asleep faster, but it can also wake me up. What exercise timing works best for my schedule and sleep habits?

 ### Phone charging in a separate room or in airplane mode starting at 10:30 pm

In addition to the sleep-disrupting blue light, smartphones are notification machines – dings, alerts, and vibrations can easily disrupt a sound night of sleep or even boost worries about next-day to-dos. I've used two workarounds with success:

Leave my phone outside of the bedroom completely. This strategy reduces the chances I will be goofing around on my phone right before bed. Plus, it's nice to wake up in the morning and not immediately check my bedside phone. I love easing into the day and being less reactive the minute I wake up.

Keep my phone in airplane mode starting at 10:30 pm. Since I now run a CGM app (instead of a receiver) on my phone, I have all audible phone notifications from other apps turned off, meaning the only sounds and vibrations I receive are from my CGM – critical for safety, but not a nuisance. I try to extend airplane mode as long as possible into the morning, maximizing low-stress quiet time before the day gets going.

BE CAUTIOUS WITH MY PHONE AROUND BEDTIME AND IN THE MORNING.

Less time tinkering in apps usually means less stress, less mental simulation before bed, and better sleep.

MY SLEEP LANDMINES

 Nighttime fear: overeating to correct a low right before bed

It's 11:30 pm, right before bed. I check my BG: 4.2 mmol/l. To be safe, I should eat something. But what and how much?

I see more overnight blood sugars in my target range when I use restraint. In this case, I'd ideally eat around 10 grams of carbs: half of an apple, 2-3 glucose tablets, a small cup of berries, etc. But so often I'm afraid of overnight lows and completely overdo the correction, only to wake up with a Landmine high at 3 am. One of my biggest errors is overeating low-carb options before bed (nuts, seeds), which can increase BG steadily and often drive me high in the middle of the night. Then I wake up tired and grumpy in the morning and my day is off to a poor start - all because I ate too much before bed.

When I successfully avoid this Landmine, it comes down to discipline: do NOT overeat to correct a low before going to sleep. As with exercise, it's useful to know how many carbs of a certain food are needed to bring my BG back to target (5.5 mmol/l). That number increases as my BG goes down further (e.g., a 2.8 mmol/l needs 15 grams of carbs), if I've had a particularly big day of exercise or many recent lows, and as insulin-on-board increases. And if I've had a lot of lows that day or not much to eat, adding some fat (a tbsp of peanut butter) or some fiber (chia seeds, a low-carb tortilla) can help prevent recurrent overnight lows.

Using CGM as the only guide to my pre-bed food correction can drive this Landmine further. CGM has some lag for low BGs, which often encourages overeating as I think about going to sleep: "Oh, I'm only at 4.3 mmol/l after eating those glucose tabs 15 minutes ago? Guess I need to eat more." If I'm low before bed, I try to confirm the CGM reading with a meter, eat the correction carbs, and then check again on the meter in 20 minutes.

WHAT HELPS ME

TRY DIFFERENT FOODS TO CORRECT BEFORE-BED LOW BGS AND FIND SOMETHING THAT I: (i) won't overeat (easy to control the quantity); (ii) can adjust to the exact level I need (roughly 5 grams of carbs raises my BG by about 1.5 mmol/l); and (iii) know will keep me in range overnight without going too high or experiencing more lows.

WHEN EXTRA WORRIED ABOUT OVERNIGHT LOWS, ADD A SMALL AMOUNT OF FAT, PROTEIN, AND FIBER TO FURTHER STABILIZE BG: 1 tbsp of peanut butter, a handful of nuts, a low-carb tortilla. This seems to help flatten my overnight BG more than eating carbs alone. However, fat and fiber will slow the absorption of carbs, so I only add them for borderline lows (4.2 mmol/l), or I delay eating them until after my BG is rising from the correction carbs.

REMEMBER THAT CGM OFTEN LAGS WHEN RECOVERING FROM LOWS. Be careful using it as the only guide to keep eating correction carbs right before bed.

Too much caffeine after 2 pm

I love Japanese green tea and enjoy strong coffee, but often make the mistake of "treating" myself too late in the day. My caffeine tolerance is pretty high, but on nights when I can't sleep, a very common cause is too much coffee or tea in the late afternoon or evening.

According to the National Sleep Foundation, caffeine hangs around in the body for more than six hours, meaning a strong cup of coffee at 2 pm can affect me well into the evening. The problem is I actually *like* the taste of these beverages, meaning I've had to find alternatives to quench my thirst.

Since I don't love plain water, I have taken to flavoring it with a fresh lemon or lime. I try not to have any green tea after 6 pm (it is lower in caffeine than coffee), and only decaf coffee after 2 pm. As noted in the food chapter, I usually drink peppermint tea after dinner or a cup of hot water with 1 tbsp of unsweetened dark chocolate cocoa powder stirred in. Both warm beverages "feel" like tea, but don't bring a big dose of caffeine that keeps me up. (Note: cocoa powder does have a tiny bit of caffeine and a related compound called theobromine, so I don't recommend this if you are highly caffeine sensitive.[38])

 WHAT HELPS ME

REDUCE OR ELIMINATE CAFFEINE CONSUMPTION 10 HOURS BEFORE BEDTIME.

Switching to tea brings less caffeine throughout the day, and herbal (non-caffeinated) tea is great as a nighttime treat without any caffeine or calories. If you are new to tea, I highly recommend going to a local tea shop or store and trying a few loose-leaf options – they taste better than most pre-bagged teas and are often cheaper overall.

SWITCH TO DECAFFEINATED COFFEE LATE IN THE DAY.

It still has *some* caffeine, but will have a much lower impact on wakefulness than normal coffee.

 ## Waking up in the morning in a completely dark room

Often in hotel rooms, I'll wake up after eight hours of sound sleep and feel completely exhausted. The same was true in my first apartment in San Francisco – my pitch black room had no windows, meaning 7:30 am looked the same as 11:30 pm. This feeling changed when I moved to an apartment with windows that let in morning light. To my surprise, it was actually easier to wake up and get moving.

I find that waking up in a completely dark room is a Landmine for feeling rested. Just as low evening light and a dark room is ideal for sound sleep, morning light is ideal for waking up.

Purchasing an alarm clock with a "wake-up light feature" helped in that uber dark bedroom in my first apartment. The device I bought, a Philips Wake-Up Light, would slowly light the whole room about 30 minutes before the alarm went off – mimicking sunrise. I still didn't jump out of bed every morning, but it was far better than waking up in a completely pitch black room. Some people online call these wake-up devices "life changing." Smart light bulbs are another option, which can be controlled from a smartphone app and set to automatically and gradually turn on based on a set time (e.g., 7 am wake-up).

The bedroom light combination is a difficult balancing act: a pitch black room is ideal for sound sleep, but may also keep helpful natural sunlight out in the morning. I've tried different combinations and settled on blinds that cover about 80% of my bedroom windows, blocking out most light at night and allowing some natural sunlight to enter in the morning. It's not pitch black, but the tradeoff works for feeling more energized in the morning. I still use the Philips Wake-Up Light, since I love the dimming option at night for reading and the additional wake-up light brightness in the morning.

WHAT HELPS ME

TRY A "GENTLE" WAKE-UP ALARM CLOCK OR A SMART LIGHT BULB to have more natural morning light in a dark room.

FIGURE OUT WHICH COMBINATION OF NIGHTTIME DARKNESS PLUS MORNING LIGHT HELPS ME SLEEP THE BEST AND WAKE UP FEELING THE MOST RESTED:

- A perfectly dark room at night and zero morning light (e.g., black out shades, an eye mask).
- A moderately dark room at night and some morning light (e.g., a wake-up alarm clock, mostly covered windows that let in some morning light).

QUESTIONS TO ASK YOURSELF

 ## Bright Spot Questions:

Think about your best nights of sleep in the past couple of weeks. What do you think made them possible? (Think broadly, including overnight BGs, food, insulin, exercise, activities before bed and during the day, bedroom setup, etc.)

If your life depended on a great night of sleep tonight, what would you do to make it happen?

How much sleep do you need to be functioning at your best? How much sleep are you actually getting?

(If you are constantly tired) What changes could you make to get an extra 30-60 minutes of sleep per night? Think more specific than "Go to bed earlier."

What small experiments or purchases (with a money back guarantee) could you try to improve your bedroom sleeping environment?

What exercise schedule puts you to sleep the fastest?

Look at the answers above. What are your Bright Spots - the things you can try to do more often? How might you encourage them?

Landmine Questions:

Think about your worst nights of sleep in the past couple of weeks. What do you think contributed?

Under what bedroom conditions do you sleep the worst - temperature, light, mattress, pillow, sounds, etc.? How does your current bedroom setup score against those conditions?

What is the #1 thing – if you avoided it every day – that would most improve your sleep?

Look at the answers above. What are your Landmines – the things you can try to do less often? How might you avoid them?

05

Tying It All
Together

WHAT'S MOST IMPORTANT TO ME?

Even after many years of living with diabetes and writing about it, I still have frustrating days when things don't go as I expect. It's a battle to do my best 24/7, but not let diabetes take over my life. I still catch myself dwelling on this morning's mistakes, or wishing I had made a different decision at dinner, or worrying about going to sleep. The default attitude is usually negative, anxious, and self-blaming.

My fondest wish is that people with diabetes take the framework from this book and apply it to their lives, putting a major emphasis on Bright Spots: What's working well in my diabetes? What behaviors and choices help keep my blood sugar in range or have a positive mental impact? What happens on my best days? How can I build routines and habits to experience more Bright Spots every day?

I get frustrated when I see vague, one-size-fits-all diabetes recommendations: eat healthy, move more, lose weight, take your medication. This generic, often finger-wagging advice misses the richness of specifics, forgets the personal component, and implies diabetes is easy. It's not!

One reason I wrote this book was to create an operating guide for my own diabetes, filled with specific, personal tactics: what are the most important Bright Spots I should be doing more often? What are the biggest Landmines I should be trying to avoid?

I like this quote from the Roman philosopher Seneca, which sums up the ultimate goal of this process:

"What is wisdom? Always desiring the same things and always refusing the same things."

Writing down my own Bright Spots and Landmines is the first step on that journey to wisdom, but it's only a start.

Living well with diabetes is about putting all my "shoulds" into action repeatedly – and ideally automatically – and that can be very difficult to do every day.

Prioritization is a good starting point: what Bright Spots and Landmines are the most impactful? What gives me the highest quality of life, and what tradeoffs am I willing to make to do better? What matters most to me? What will be easiest to try?

If there were only five tactics I could choose from this book, they would be:

1 Eat less than 30 grams of carbohydrates at one time.

Carbohydrates are the biggest driver of blood sugar spikes; reducing them takes out the biggest variable in my diabetes, keeps me much safer when dosing insulin, cuts my stress and worry, and lets me put diabetes in the background.

2 Check BG 2-3 hours after a meal (or wear CGM) to make course corrections and learn what foods work for me.

Glucose monitoring is the best way to learn what works and to guide safer diabetes driving, especially after meals. It is the clear windshield on the front of my car; without it, I'm far less likely to stay on the road (in range).

3 Remember why an in-range blood sugar benefits me TODAY: better mood, relationships, energy to do things that make me happy.

The WHY in diabetes is critical, and "avoid long-term complications" is not the best motivator. Complications are definitely scary, but they are also vague, far away, negative, and often not a compelling reason to make a different decision right now. In fact, I can rationalize my way out of making good decisions very easily: "Yes, that brownie looks good. What's the harm in just one? I'll get back on track tomorrow." Finding positive TODAY reasons to take care of my diabetes and health makes a tremendous difference.

④ BG numbers are not "good" or "bad"; they are just information to make a decision.

Feeling graded on every BG drives guilt, frustration, failure, and checking BG less often. Not every number has a simple cause and effect relationship, so I can't blame myself when I'm out of range. Changing the context around each BG – useful information to make a decision – has helped me embrace the numbers as a positive, welcome partner.

⑤ Use productive, uplifting questions instead of deflating, negative, blaming questions.

Asking productive questions is the gateway drug to doing better with diabetes. There is something new to learn about this disease every day, since life is constantly changing. Approaching diabetes with a voracious sense of curiosity works wonders for doing better: How can I learn from this? What can I do right now to improve? What can I change next time?

I find this utterly fascinating: two of my five critical Diabetes Bright Spots are focused on food, and the other three focus on mindset. This is going to be different for every person, but one thing is clear for me: mindset goes a long way.

One of my diabetes heroes, psychologist Dr. Bill Polonsky, talks a lot about the "Something Clicked" study: How do some people go from struggling with diabetes to doing better? What clicked? He says there are five things:

1. A new perspective.
2. A friend who cares.
3. A healthcare provider who cares.
4. A new effective treatment.
5. Getting complications.

And once something clicks, how do people stay on track?

1. Remember why you should even bother.
2. Develop a concrete, doable plan for action.
3. Don't do diabetes alone.
4. Participate in diabetes research.

I see two common themes in those lists: how I think about diabetes (mindset) and who is on my team (support) matter a great deal. That gives me tremendous hope, since those are both resources I can access and change today. I can go to my loved ones or to the diabetes online community right now to find support. I can change my perspective on diabetes in this moment.

As I wrote this book, I talked to many people living well with diabetes, particularly those with decades more experience than me. Many shared that their need for support has grown over time. "Support" could come from the online community, the offline community, a loved one, or working with a caring healthcare provider. The point is worth emphasizing:

DON'T **DO DIABETES ALONE.**

Even still, diabetes can often feel like an unfair drive: no idea what address I'm going to, battling ice and hail on the roads every day, and flat tires left and right. If this book has one message, it's that we can all find an address to guide us TODAY, tactics to drive safer, and co-pilots to support us. Reaching our destination, of course, will never be easy. As psychologist Dr. Gordon Livingston puts it in his great book *Too Soon Old, Too Late Smart:*

"Virtually all the happiness–producing processes in our lives take time, usually a long time: learning new things, changing old behaviors, building satisfying relationships, raising children. This is why patience and determination are among life's primary virtues."

The right mentality has been a great asset on my own journey: "I will figure this out. I will never stop learning and experimenting. I will not let diabetes hold me back. I will make the most of my time here on Earth, even though I have to bring diabetes with me."

I have a welcome mat at my front door that provides a succinct reminder:

I smile every time I see it, since it embeds many lessons that I often forget:

- I cannot control everything in my life, but I can always control my response to it.
- Take it one day at a time.
- Have fun!

This Sanskrit proverb (courtesy of *The Time Paradox*) puts it even more beautifully:

Yesterday is already a dream
And tomorrow but a vision
But today well lived makes every yesterday a
dream of happiness
And every tomorrow a vision of hope.

For me, Bright Spots and Landmines have enabled me to live well today, to reflect more happily on yesterday, and to have hope for a better future.

I wish the very same for you.

Find Your Bright Spots

What is going well in my diabetes? What am I doing right that I should try to do more often?

What happens on my *best* days with diabetes?

What do I eat?	What does my diabetes self-talk sound like?	When and how do I exercise?
How did I sleep the night before?	What do loved ones do that is helpful?	If I wanted to have one of these Bright Spot days today, what would I do to make it happen?

What times of day or days of the week is my glucose consistently staying in range (4-8 mmol/l or 4-10 mmol/l, depending on your preferences)? What choices might be enabling that to happen?

What is one Bright Spot decision from the past week, that if repeated consistently, would improve my quality of life?

What are some small steps that I could take this week to increase my Diabetes Bright Spots? What am I willing to try?

Identify Your Landmines

What happens on my most *challenging* days with diabetes?

What do I eat?

What does my diabetes self-talk sound like?

Do I exercise?

How did I sleep the night before?

What do loved ones do that is unhelpful?

If I wanted to avoid having one of these Diabetes Landmine days today, what is the #1 thing I would steer clear of?

What times of day or days of the week does my glucose always seem to go out of range (less than 4 or over 11 mmol/l)? What choices might be driving that to happen?

What is one diabetes decision from the past week that I wish I could re-do? How would I have made a different choice?

What are some small steps that I could take this week to avoid my Diabetes Landmines? What am I willing to try?

My Diabetes Bright Spots

What am I doing well that I should keep doing?
What happens on my best days with diabetes?

1
2
3
4
5

To experience these Diabetes Bright Spots more
often, I need to:

1
2
3
4
5

My Diabetes Landmines

What decisions always seem to explode into out-of-range blood sugars (less than 4 or over 11 mmol/l)? What happens on my most challenging days with diabetes?

1

2

3

4

5

To avoid these Diabetes Landmines, I need to:

1

2

3

4

5

BOOK SUMMARY:
MY BRIGHT SPOTS & LANDMINES

 Food

MY BRIGHT SPOTS

- Eat less than 30 grams of carbohydrates at one time
- Choose breakfast foods high in protein, fat, and fiber (e.g., chia pudding, eggs)
- Check BG 2–3 hours after meals (or wear CGM) to learn what foods work and make course corrections
- Fill half of my plate with vegetables
- Dose insulin 20 minutes before eating a meal with 30 grams of carbs or more
- Eat an early dinner more than three hours before bedtime, no snacking afterwards
- Cook at home instead of eating out
- In restaurants, order vegetables to replace normal side dishes
- Eat berries instead of traditional desserts
- Snack on nuts and seeds
- Ask: "Am I actually hungry, or am I just bored, tired, or near food?"
- Eat slowly and stop before I'm 100% full
- View food purchases like a political vote: what kind of organization am I supporting?

MY LANDMINES

- Hypoglycemia binge: overeating to correct a low or using it as an excuse to "treat myself"
- White foods: bread, potatoes, rice, noodles, baked goods, crackers, chips, sugar
- Junk food in the house, snacks in sight, eating directly out of the package
- Packaged foods with more than 10 ingredients and high doses of sugar ("foodlike substances")
- Sugary drinks: fruit smoothies, big bottles of juice, regular soda, sweet tea, milkshakes, sports drinks
- Too many exceptions ("Just this once!") and excuses ("I earned it!")

 # Mindset

MY BRIGHT SPOTS

- Why does an in-range blood sugar benefit me TODAY: better mood, relationships, energy levels
- BG numbers are neutral information to make a decision; they are not "good" or "bad" grades or "tests"
- Rely on loved ones and friends for support, remember my diabetes affects them too, and communicate about what is helpful
- Gratitude for what I have and how far diabetes has come; I

have a duty to take care of myself
- Take 5-10 minutes for deep breaths in the morning (mindfulness)
- Use the "zoom out" visualization to put stress into perspective. Will I remember this moment in a year?
- Change my immediate environment to make better choices easier or unhelpful choices harder
- Set process goals with mini-milestones: focus on consistency and routine, not outcomes
- There are only 24 hours in a day and I can only do my best
- Commit to a goal and hold myself accountable: tell friends, make it public, lock myself in financially

MY LANDMINES

- Perfectionist mindset, unrealistic BG expectations, obsessing about things I cannot control
- Unproductive, deflating, blaming questions: Why am I so terrible at this? Why is this not working? Could diabetes be any worse? How could I make the same mistake again?

╟╢ Exercise

MY BRIGHT SPOTS

- Walk, especially after meals and to correct a high BG
- What is my BG now? How much do I expect it to change by the time I finish activity? Should I eat or take insulin?

- Choose activities I find fun and actually want to do. Am I looking forward to exercise tomorrow?
- Find the right before-exercise glucose target, and learn how many carbs are needed to raise BG to that target
- Store treatments for low BGs everywhere in my life (glucose tabs), and always carry them during exercise
- Reduce bolus insulin based on activity type (e.g., -75% for endurance exercise, -30% before walking)
- Track activity with a device or an app to add motivation and friendly competition
- Listen to podcasts, audiobooks, or watch something entertaining during exercise
- Schedule activity: "I lift weights on Monday, Wednesday, and Friday mornings. I ride my bike on Tuesday, Thursday, and Sunday afternoons."
- Eliminate the barriers to exercise with home workouts and exercise apps
- Accountability to an exercise partner, class, or club
- Adopt a dog: I MUST move!

MY LANDMINES

- "All or nothing" mentality: "Well, I don't have an hour, so I can't exercise"
- Eating too close to starting exercise: low BG during activity, high BG after activity
- Overeating after exercise
- Poor recovery: failing to stretch, not enough water, not enough sleep
- Focusing on how painful exercise feels while doing it

 # Sleep

MY BRIGHT SPOTS

- At least 7 hours of sleep: more next-day BGs in range, less insulin, more energy, better mood, less hunger
- Overnight BGs in a tight range (4.5-8 mmol/l): early dinner, no snacking, disciplined bedtime corrections
- Glucose tablets next to my bed: no refrigerator eating, less disrupted sleep
- Limit light exposure at night, and use an app/device setting to limit blue screen light
- Invest in a better mattress and pillow and do not settle for uncomfortable sleep
- Cooler room temperature (65 degrees) and a lighter blanket
- Morning or afternoon exercise to fall asleep faster
- Phone charging in a separate room or in airplane mode starting at 10:30 pm

MY LANDMINES

- Nighttime fear: overeating right before bed
- Too much caffeine after 2pm
- Waking up in the morning in a completely dark room

GRATITUDE

This book has been an immensely gratifying journey that would not have happened without many phenomenal people.

I'm thankful for all the brilliant minds who provided feedback and advice on this book's ideas and writing, including (in alphabetical order) Dr. Zach Bloomgarden, Dr. Bruce Buckingham, Nancy Crane, Ashley Dartnell, Dr. Daniel De Salvo, David Edelman, Dr. Steve Edelman, Felicia Gelsey, Jeff Halpern, Dr. Nate Heintzmann, Manny Hernandez, Dr. Irl Hirsch, Jeff Hitchcock, Dr. Philip Home, Carl Rashad Jaeger, Christie Jensen, Dr. Nicole Johnson, Scott Johnson, Andrew Jones, Dr. Fran Kaufman, Dr. Aaron Kowalski, Davida Kruger, Dr. Jake Kushner, Dr. Robin Lie, Sarita Lisa, Sarah Lucas, Dr. Trang Ly, Steve Mallinson, Peter Nerothin, Dr. Anne Peters, Dr. Jeremy Pettus, Gina Reeves, Lauren Reifsnyder, Kyle Rose, Blair Ryan, James Shirk, Phil Southerland, Kerri Sparling, Sandy Struss, Ginger Vieira, Dr. Jill Weissberg-Benchell, and Gloria Yee. I'm so sorry if I forgot anyone!

Thank you to the amazing, brilliant teams at The diaTribe Foundation (Amelia Dmowska, Mallory Erickson, Emily Fitts, Jeemin Kwon, Ben Pallant, Emma Ryan) and Close Concerns (Ann Carracher, Abigail Dove, Hannah Duncan, Veronica Hash, Brian Levine, Payal Marathe, Maeve Serino)! For this mmol/l version, a special thanks to our incredibly helpful Dartmouth Fellows, Amanda Jiang and Anna Nguyen.

I'm also deeply grateful to The diaTribe Foundation Board of Directors – Dennis Boyle, Jeff Halpern, Dr. Orville Kolterman, and Ruth Owades – for sharing so many ideas and believing in this project from the start.

The masterful Jim Hirsch gave me confidence to pursue this book when it was just an idea, and gave further wind to my sails when it was just one chapter and a cobbled together introduction. Jim, thank you for the phenomenal editing and writing advice every step of the way.

I would be nowhere in my diabetes career without the support and encouragement of John and Kelly Close, who founded The diaTribe Foundation in 2013 and Close Concerns in 2002. They have given me more responsibility than anyone my age can ask for, and are two of the kindest, wisest, and most thoughtful people I have ever met. John and Kelly took a chance on me as a summer intern six years ago, graciously offered me a full-time job, and have supported me in every conceivable way since – including starting my column, Adam's Corner, four years ago. I hope one day I can have one-tenth of the impact on the diabetes world that you have had.

To Mom, Victoria, AJ, Tristan, Jack, Molly, Linda, and Glenn: thank you for never letting diabetes hold me back. I'm so thankful to have grown up in such a loving, supportive household. All of you inspire me to do better, to be more empathetic, and to make the world a better place.

To Priscilla and Sencha, your unwavering support is one of the key reasons this book actually came to be. Sencha, there's something about your wagging tail that just puts a smile on my face and a spring in my step – no matter how many Diabetes Landmines I've had that day. Priscilla, you were a direct inspiration for so many Bright Spots in this book, and your kindness and masterful visual design illuminates every single page. This project would not exist without your encouragement and patience in the face of my endless second-guessing. You never flinched at my chia seed concoctions (okay, maybe a little bit), or my grumpy high BG moods, or our late-night dinner walks. Thank you for making every single hour with you a Bright Spot. You are the most loving, kindest, generous, and funniest person I've ever known. Luffya!

ADAM'S CORNER COLUMNS ON DIATRIBE

FOOD

---

10 Diet Commandments for Better Diabetes Management
diatribe.org/10-diet-commandments-better-diabetes-management

Low Carb vs. High Carb - My Surprising 24-day Diabetes Diet Battle
diatribe.org/low-carb-vs-high-carb-my-surprising-24-day-diabetes-diet-battle

Low Carb vs. High Carb II – My Diabetes Diet Battle Continued
diatribe.org/low-carb-vs-high-carb-ii-my-diabetes-diet-battle-continued

Your Questions Answered: Low Carb vs. High Carb
diatribe.org/your-questions-answered-low-carb-vs-high-carb

Diabetes on a 65% Fat Diet, Chia for Breakfast, and Intermittent Fasting
diatribe.org/diabetes-65-fat-diet-chia-breakfast-intermittent-fasting

How to Thrive in a Toxic Food Environment that Encourages Bad Choices
diatribe.org/issues/64/adams-corner

What I Actually Eat - Taking My Diabetes Diet Commandments into Daily Life
diatribe.org/what-i-actually-eat-taking-my-diabetes-diet-commandments-daily-life

A Home Run Breakfast with Diabetes
diatribe.org/home-run-breakfast-diabetes

Are all carbohydrates created equal?
diatribe.org/issues/58/adams-corner

Beating Challenging Meals and Winter Weather
diatribe.org/issues/60/adams-corner

EXERCISE

The Step-by-Step Approach to Better Blood Sugars: Walking
diatribe.org/issues/51/adams-corner

Get in the Zone: My Tips For Avoiding Hypoglycemia During Exercise
diatribe.org/get-zone-my-tips-avoiding-hypoglycemia-during-exercise

Diabetes & Exercise Solutions – No Time, Too Expensive, Painful, Boring, Unmotivated
diatribe.org/diabetes-exercise-solutions-part-i-no-time-too-expensive-painful-boring-unmotivated

How Much Activity Do You Actually Get? Why Activity Tracking Is Worth It, and Perhaps Needed More Than Ever
diatribe.org/issues/72/adams-corner

OTHER TOPICS

How many factors actually affect blood glucose?
diatribe.org/factors

10 Tips for Teenagers to Live Well with Diabetes
diatribe.org/10-tips-teenagers-live-well-type-1-diabetes

What are your "Diabetes Landmines?" The Seven Mistakes I Always Make and What I Learned Trying to Avoid Them
diatribe.org/issues/70/adams-corner

Getting to Goal – The Four Biggest Game-changers for Improving My Diabetes Management
diatribe.org/issues/66/adams-corner

Can Getting More Sleep Improve Blood Sugar Control? What One Month of Tracking My Sleep Revealed
diatribe.org/issues/53/adams-corner

REFERENCES

1. Chip and Dan Heath, *Switch: How to Change Things When Change is Hard* (New York: Random House, 2010).

2. Barbara Fredrickson, *Positivity: Top-Notch Research Reveals the Upward Spiral That Will Change Your Life* (New York: Random House, 2009).

3. Feinman et al., "Dietary carbohydrate restriction as the first approach in diabetes management: Critical review and evidence base," *Nutrition*, 2015, **http://www.nutritionjrnl. com/article/S0899-9007(14)00332-3/pdf** (accessed on August 15, 2016).

4. Jeff Volek and Stephen Phinney, *The Art and Science of Low Carbohydrate Living* (Beyond Obesity: 2011).

5. Adam Brown, "Diabetes on a 65% Fat Diet, Chia for Breakfast, and Intermittent Fasting," *diaTribe*, 2016, **https://diatribe.org/diabetes-65-fat-diet-chia-breakfast-intermittent-fasting** (accessed on October 31, 2016).

6. Bolli and Gerich, "The 'dawn phenomenon'--a common occurrence in both non-insulin-dependent and insulin-dependent diabetes mellitus," *New England Journal of Medicine*, 1984, **http://www.nejm.org/doi/full/10.1056/NEJM198403223101203** (accessed on November 30, 2016); Carroll and Schade, "The dawn phenomenon revisited: implications for diabetes therapy," *Endocrine Practice*, 2005, **http://dx.doi.org/10.4158/EP.11.1.55** (accessed on November 30, 2016); Freckmann et al., "The Circadian Study," *Diabetes Care*, 2008, **http://care.diabetesjournals.org/content/31/11/e85.long** (accessed on November 30, 2016).

7. Peter Whoriskey, "Government revises Dietary Guidelines for Americans: Go ahead and have some eggs," *Washington Post*, 2016, **https://www.washingtonpost.com/news/wonk/wp/ 2016/01/07/government-revises- dietary-guidelines-for-americans-go-ahead-and-have-some-eggs/** (accessed November 1, 2016); U.S. Department of Health and Human Services and U.S. Department of Agriculture, "2015-2020 Dietary Guidelines for Americans: 8th Edition," 2015, **http://health.gov/dietaryguidelines/2015/guidelines/** (accessed October 15, 2016); Cleveland Clinic, "Why You Should No Longer Worry About Cholesterol in Food," 2015, **https://health.clevelandclinic.org/2015/02/why-you-should-no-longer-worry-about-cholester ol-in-food/** (accessed October 15, 2016).

8. These are typically sold in grocery stores or can be purchased here: **www.latortilla factory.com/product/low-carb-high-fiber-tortillas-made-whole-wheat-original-size/**

9. James Lane, "Caffeine, Glucose Metabolism, and Type 2 Diabetes," *Journal of Caffeine Research*, 2011, **http://online.liebertpub.com/doi/pdfplus/10.1089/jcr.2010.0007** (accessed on February 6, 2017).

10. Susana Guerrero, "Only 4 percent of Americans are eating enough vegetables," *SF Gate*, 2015, **http://www.sfgate.com/news/article/Only-4-Percent-of-Americans-Are- Eating-Enough-6642245.php** (accessed on August 12, 2016); National Fruit and Vegetable

Alliance, "2015 National Action Plan Report Card," 2015, **http://www.nfva.org/national action_plan.html** (accessed August 12, 2016).

11. Modified from "Red Wine Vinaigrette Quick Salad Dressing," **https://recipes.heart.org/Recipes/1228/Red-Wine-Vinaigrette-Quick-Salad-Dressing** (accessed on January 30, 2017).

12. Cobry et al., "Timing of Meal Insulin Boluses to Achieve Optimal Postprandial Glycemic Control in Patients with Type 1 Diabetes," *Diabetes Technology & Therapeutics*, 2010, **http://online.liebertpub.com/doi/abs/10.1089/dia.2009.0112** (accessed on November 29, 2016).

13. "Food Waste in America." *Feeding America.* **http://www.feedingamerica.org/about-us/how-we-work/securing-meals/reducing-food-waste.html** (accessed on January 8, 2017).

14. Gary Scheiner, "Pramlintide Applied: Practical Tips for Getting Symlin to Work Right," *diaTribe*, 2010, **https://diatribe.org/pramlintide-applied-practical-tips-getting-symlin-work-right** (accessed on October 1, 2016).

15. "Understanding satiety: feeling full after a meal," British Nutrition Foundation, 2013, **https://www.nutrition.org.uk/healthyliving/fuller/understanding-satiety-feeling-full-after-a-meal.html** (accessed on October 1, 2016).

16. "Flours and Nut Meals," Bob's Red Mill, **http://www.bobsredmill.com/shop/flours-and-meals.html** (accessed on November 30, 2016).

17. Michael Pollan, *Food Rules: An Eater's Manual* (New York: Penguin Books, 2009).

18. Steele et al., "Ultra-processed foods and added sugars in the US diet: evidence from a nationally representative cross-sectional study," *BMJ Open*, 2016, **http://bmjopen.bmj.com/content/6/3/e009892** (accessed on October 15, 2016).

19. US Food & Drug Administration, "Final Determination Regarding Partially Hydrogenated Oils (Removing Trans Fat)," 2016, **http://www.fda.gov/Food/Ingredients PackagingLabeling/FoodAdditivesIngredients/ucm449162.htm** (accessed on November 26, 2016); Harvard School of Public Health, "Shining the Spotlight on Trans Fats," **https://www.hsph.harvard.edu/nutritionsource/transfats/** (accessed on November 26, 2016); Matthew Herper, "FDA Bans Trans Fats. Hooray!" Forbes, 2015, **http://www.forbes.com/sites/matthewherper/2015/06/16/why-the-fdas-trans-fat-ban-is-a-triumph-of-good-government/#4aea233d2620** (accessed on November 26, 2016); Mozaffarian et al., "Trans Fatty Acids and Cardiovascular Disease," *New England Journal of Medicine*, 2006, **http://www.nejm.org/doi/full/10.1056/NEJMra054035** (accessed on November 26, 2016).

20. Estruch et al., "Primary Prevention of Cardiovascular Disease with a Mediterranean Diet," *New England Journal of Medicine*, 2013, **http://www.nejm.org/doi/full/10.1056/NEJMoa1200303#t=article** (accessed on November 26, 2016); Emilio Ros, "Nuts and CVD," *British Journal of Nutrition*, 2015, **https://www.ncbi.nlm.nih.gov/pubmed/26148914** (accessed on November 26, 2016); Guasch-Ferré et al., "Olive oil intake and risk of cardiovascular disease and mortality in the PREDIMED Study," *BMC Medicine*, 2014, **https://www.ncbi.nlm.nih.gov/pubmed/24886626** (accessed on November 26, 2016); Guasch-Ferré et al., "Frequency of nut consumption and mortality risk in the PREDIMED nutrition intervention trial," *BMC Medicine*, 2014, **https://www.ncbi.nlm.nih.gov/pmc/articles/PMC3738153/** (accessed on November 26, 2016); Bao et al., "Association of Nut Consumption with Total and Cause-Specific Mortality," *New England Journal of Medicine*, 2014, **https://www.ncbi.nlm.nih.gov/pmc/articles/PMC3931001/** (accessed on November 26, 2016).

21. "Ask the Experts: Hydrogenated Oils," Berkeley Wellness, 2011, **http://www.berkeley wellness.com/healthy-eating/food/article/hydrogenated-oils** (accessed on November 30, 2016).

22. Ahmed et al., "Sugar addiction: pushing the drug–sugar analogy to the limit," *Curr Opin Clin Nutr Metab Care*, 2013, **https://www.ncbi.nlm.nih.gov/pubmed/?term=Sugar+ addiction%3A+pushing+the+drug- sugar+analogy+to+the+limit** (accessed on November 26, 2016); James J. DiNicolantonio and Sean C. Lucan, "Sugar Season. It's Everywhere, and Addictive." *The New York Times*, 2014, **http://www.nytimes.com/2014/12/23/opinion/ sugar-season-its-everywhere-and-addictive.html?_r=1** (accessed on November 26, 2016).

23. Suez et al., "Artificial sweeteners induce glucose intolerance by altering the gut microbiota," *Nature*, 2014, **http://www.nature.com/nature/journal/vaop/ncurrent/pdf/ nature13793.pdf** (accessed on November 26, 2016); Wang et al., "Sucralose Promotes Food Intake through NPY and a Neuronal Fasting Response," *Cell Metabolism*, 2016, **http://www.cell.com/cell-metabolism/abstract/S1550-4131(16)30296-0** (accessed on November 26, 2016); Bret Stetka, "How Artificial Sweeteners May Cause Us to Eat More," *Scientific American*, 2016, **http://www.scientificamerican.com/article/how- artificial-sweeteners-may-cause-us-to-eat-more/** (accessed on November 26, 2016). **http://www.scientificamerican.com/article/how-artificial-sweeteners-may-cause-us-to-eat- more/** (accessed on November 26, 2016).

24. Brenè Brown, *The Gifts of Imperfection: Let Go of Who You Think You're Supposed to Be and Embrace Who You Are* (Hazelden: Minnesota, 2010).

25. Adam Brown and Kelly Close, "The diaTribe advisory board on what every person with diabetes must know," *diaTribe*, 2012, **https://diatribe.org/issues/50/diabetes-dialogue** (accessed July 1, 2016).

26. For more on the discovery of insulin and the treatment options just prior, see *Breakthrough: Elizabeth Hughes, the Discovery of Insulin, and the Making of a Medical Miracle* by Thea Cooper and Arthur Ainsberg; *The Discovery of Insulin* by Michael Bliss; and *The Fight to Survive: A Young Girl, Diabetes, and the Discovery of Insulin* by Caroline Cox.

27. "Giving thanks can make you happier," Harvard Health, 2011, **http://www.health. harvard.edu/healthbeat/giving-thanks-can-make-you-happier** (accessed December 15, 2016).

28. Olivia Fox Cabane, *The Charisma Myth: How Anyone Can Master the Art and Science of Personal Magnetism* (New York: Penguin Group: 2012)

29. BJ Fogg, "BJ's note: March 2, 2014 12:10pm," **http://tinyhabits.com/sandbox/** (accessed on December 2, 2016).

30. Big Blue Test Program Email Communication, Diabetes Hands Foundation, October 21, 2016.

31. Dr. Len Kravitz, "High–Intensity Interval Training," American College of Sports Medicine, 2014, **https://www.acsm.org/docs/brochures/high-intensity-interval-training.pdf** (accessed on November 26, 2016).

32. Esther Wu, Tiffany Kha, Adam Brown, and Kelly Close, "How Did Alasdair Wilkins Lose 100 lbs in a Year?" *diaTribe*, 2015, **http://www.diatribe.org/how-did-alasdair-wilkins-lose- 100-lbs-year** (accessed on December 15, 2016).

33. Stephen Covey, *The 7 Habits of Highly Effective People: Powerful Lessons in Personal Change* (New York: Simon & Schuster, 2013).

34. Jeff Volek and Stephen Phinney, *The Art and Science of Low Carbohydrate Living* (Beyond Obesity: 2011).

35. Denic-Roberts et al., "Subjective sleep disturbances and glycemic control in adults with long-standing type 1 diabetes: The Pittsburgh's Epidemiology of Diabetes Complications study," *Diabetes Res Clin Pract*, 2016, **https://www.ncbi.nlm.nih.gov/ pubmed/27415404** (accessed on January 13, 2017); Donga et al., "Partial Sleep Restriction Decreases Insulin Sensitivity in Type 1 Diabetes," *Diabetes Care*, 2010, **https://www.ncbi.nlm.nih.gov/pmc/articles/PMC2890361/** (accessed on January 13, 2017); Donga et al., "A single night of partial sleep deprivation induces insulin resistance in multiple metabolic pathways in healthy subjects," *J Clin Endocrinol Metab*, 2010, **https://www.ncbi.nlm.nih.gov/pubmed/20371664** (accessed on January 13, 2017); Karen et al., "Role of sleep quality in the metabolic syndrome," *Diabetes Metab Syndr Obes*, 2016, **https://www.ncbi.nlm.nih.gov/pmc/articles/PMC5003523/** (accessed on January 13, 2017); Knutson et al., "Role of sleep duration and quality in the risk and severity of type 2 diabetes mellitus.," *Arch Intern Med*, 2006, **https://www.ncbi.nlm.nih.gov/pubmed/16983057** (accessed on January 13, 2017); Markwald et al., "Impact of insufficient sleep on total daily energy expenditure, food intake, and weight gain," *PNAS*, 2013, **http://www.pnas.org/ content/110/14/5695.abstract** (accessed on January 13, 2017); Arora and Taheri, "Sleep Optimization and Diabetes Control: A Review of the Literature," *Diabetes Ther*, 2015, **https://www.ncbi.nlm.nih.gov/pmc/articles/PMC4674464/** (accessed on January 13, 2017).

36. Reutrakul and Van Cauter, "Interactions between sleep, circadian function, and glucose metabolism: implications for risk and severity of diabetes," *Annals of the New York Academy of Sciences*, 2014, **http://onlinelibrary.wiley.com/doi/10.1111/nyas.12355/epdf** (accessed on January 13, 2017).

37. "Touch: A Great Night's Sleep Can Depend on the Comfort You Feel in Your Bedroom Environment," National Sleep Foundation, 2012,**https://sleepfoundation.org/bedroom/touch.php** (accessed on December 15, 2016).

38. "Cocoa, dry powder, unsweetened," Self NutritionData, **http://nutritiondata.self.com/ facts/sweets/5471/2** (accessed on January 27, 2016).

ABOUT

ADAM BROWN, diagnosed with diabetes in 2001, is a Senior Editor at *diaTribe* and leads Diabetes Technology & Digital Health at Close Concerns. Adam writes and speaks extensively about diabetes and chronic disease, and at age 28, is recognized as a leading expert in diabetes technology. Adam is a widely requested speaker and has shared a patient perspective at numerous venues since 2010, including local and international conferences, FDA and NIH meetings, and the field's largest scientific gatherings. He graduated summa cum laude from the Wharton School of the University of Pennsylvania in 2011 as a Joseph Wharton and Benjamin Franklin Scholar. Adam spends his free time outside in San Francisco drinking tea, hiking with his girlfriend Priscilla, and teaching his old dog new tricks.

The diaTribe Foundation was founded in 2013 by Kelly L. Close, who has lived with diabetes for over 30 years. As a tax-exempt 501(c)3 non-profit, its goal is to improve the lives of people with diabetes and prediabetes and to advocate for action. *diaTribe*'s origins date back to 2006 with the creation of the *diaTribe* newsletter. Beginning as a fully volunteer effort, *diaTribe* was and continues to be a mission-focused organization driven by compassion and empathy. Its purpose is to provide content that helps people touched by diabetes live healthier, happier, or more hopeful lives. Find out more at **diatribe.org/foundation**.

Lightning Source UK Ltd.
Milton Keynes UK
UKHW052232220919
350157UK00017B/184/P